Nail Technician Exam

SECRETS

Study Guide
Your Key to Exam Success

NT Test Review for the
Nail Technician Exam

Dear Future Exam Success Story:

First of all, **THANK YOU** for purchasing Mometrix study materials!

Second, congratulations! You are one of the few determined test-takers who are committed to doing whatever it takes to excel on your exam. **You have come to the right place.** We developed these study materials with one goal in mind: to deliver you the information you need in a format that's concise and easy to use.

In addition to optimizing your guide for the content of the test, we've outlined our recommended steps for breaking down the preparation process into small, attainable goals so you can make sure you stay on track.

We've also analyzed the entire test-taking process, identifying the most common pitfalls and showing how you can overcome them and be ready for any curveball the test throws you.

Standardized testing is one of the biggest obstacles on your road to success, which only increases the importance of doing well in the high-pressure, high-stakes environment of test day. Your results on this test could have a significant impact on your future, and this guide provides the information and practical advice to help you achieve your full potential on test day.

Your success is our success

We would love to hear from you! If you would like to share the story of your exam success or if you have any questions or comments in regard to our products, please contact us at **800-673-8175** or **support@mometrix.com**.

Thanks again for your business and we wish you continued success!

Sincerely,
The Mometrix Test Preparation Team

Need more help? Check out our flashcards at:
http://MometrixFlashcards.com/NailTechnician

Copyright © 2019 by Mometrix Media LLC. All rights reserved.
Written and edited by the Mometrix Exam Secrets Test Prep Team
Printed in the United States of America

TABLE OF CONTENTS

INTRODUCTION 1

SECRET KEY #1 – PLAN BIG, STUDY SMALL 2
    INFORMATION ORGANIZATION 2
    TIME MANAGEMENT 2
    STUDY ENVIRONMENT 2

SECRET KEY #2 – MAKE YOUR STUDYING COUNT 3
    RETENTION 3
    MODALITY 3

SECRET KEY #3 – PRACTICE THE RIGHT WAY 4
    PRACTICE TEST STRATEGY 5

SECRET KEY #4 – PACE YOURSELF 6

SECRET KEY #5 – HAVE A PLAN FOR GUESSING 7
    WHEN TO START THE GUESSING PROCESS 7
    HOW TO NARROW DOWN THE CHOICES 8
    WHICH ANSWER TO CHOOSE 9

TEST-TAKING STRATEGIES 10
    QUESTION STRATEGIES 10
    ANSWER CHOICE STRATEGIES 11
    GENERAL STRATEGIES 12
    FINAL NOTES 13

SCIENTIFIC CONCEPTS 15
    INFECTION CONTROL 15
    SKIN ANATOMY & PHYSIOLOGY 21
    NAIL ANATOMY AND PHYSIOLOGY 26
    BASIC CHEMISTRY AND PRODUCT FUNCTION 31

NAIL TECHNOLOGY PROCEDURES 48
    GENERAL PROCEDURES 48
    EQUIPMENT AND SUPPLIES 50
    NAIL SERVICE PREPARATION 51
    MANICURE SERVICES 53
    PEDICURE SERVICES 58
    MASSAGE 62
    NAIL ENHANCEMENT 66

NAIL TECHNICIAN PRACTICE TEST 87

ANSWER KEY AND EXPLANATIONS 94

HOW TO OVERCOME TEST ANXIETY 100
    CAUSES OF TEST ANXIETY 100
    ELEMENTS OF TEST ANXIETY 101
    EFFECTS OF TEST ANXIETY 101
    PHYSICAL STEPS FOR BEATING TEST ANXIETY 102
    MENTAL STEPS FOR BEATING TEST ANXIETY 103
    STUDY STRATEGY 104
    TEST TIPS 106

    IMPORTANT QUALIFICATION 107
THANK YOU **108**
ADDITIONAL BONUS MATERIAL **109**

Introduction

Thank you for purchasing this resource! You have made the choice to prepare yourself for a test that could have a huge impact on your future, and this guide is designed to help you be fully ready for test day. Obviously, it's important to have a solid understanding of the test material, but you also need to be prepared for the unique environment and stressors of the test, so that you can perform to the best of your abilities.

For this purpose, the first section that appears in this guide is the **Secret Keys**. We've devoted countless hours to meticulously researching what works and what doesn't, and we've boiled down our findings to the five most impactful steps you can take to improve your performance on the test. We start at the beginning with study planning and move through the preparation process, all the way to the testing strategies that will help you get the most out of what you know when you're finally sitting in front of the test.

We recommend that you start preparing for your test as far in advance as possible. However, if you've bought this guide as a last-minute study resource and only have a few days before your test, we recommend that you skip over the first two Secret Keys since they address a long-term study plan.

If you struggle with **test anxiety**, we strongly encourage you to check out our recommendations for how you can overcome it. Test anxiety is a formidable foe, but it can be beaten, and we want to make sure you have the tools you need to defeat it.

Secret Key #1 – Plan Big, Study Small

There's a lot riding on your performance. If you want to ace this test, you're going to need to keep your skills sharp and the material fresh in your mind. You need a plan that lets you review everything you need to know while still fitting in your schedule. We'll break this strategy down into three categories.

Information Organization

Start with the information you already have: the official test outline. From this, you can make a complete list of all the concepts you need to cover before the test. Organize these concepts into groups that can be studied together, and create a list of any related vocabulary you need to learn so you can brush up on any difficult terms. You'll want to keep this vocabulary list handy once you actually start studying since you may need to add to it along the way.

Time Management

Once you have your set of study concepts, decide how to spread them out over the time you have left before the test. Break your study plan into small, clear goals so you have a manageable task for each day and know exactly what you're doing. Then just focus on one small step at a time. When you manage your time this way, you don't need to spend hours at a time studying. Studying a small block of content for a short period each day helps you retain information better and avoid stressing over how much you have left to do. You can relax knowing that you have a plan to cover everything in time. In order for this strategy to be effective though, you have to start studying early and stick to your schedule. Avoid the exhaustion and futility that comes from last-minute cramming!

Study Environment

The environment you study in has a big impact on your learning. Studying in a coffee shop, while probably more enjoyable, is not likely to be as fruitful as studying in a quiet room. It's important to keep distractions to a minimum. You're only planning to study for a short block of time, so make the most of it. Don't pause to check your phone or get up to find a snack. It's also important to **avoid multitasking**. Research has consistently shown that multitasking will make your studying dramatically less effective. Your study area should also be comfortable and well-lit so you don't have the distraction of straining your eyes or sitting on an uncomfortable chair.

The time of day you study is also important. You want to be rested and alert. Don't wait until just before bedtime. Study when you'll be most likely to comprehend and remember. Even better, if you know what time of day your test will be, set that time aside for study. That way your brain will be used to working on that subject at that specific time and you'll have a better chance of recalling information.

Finally, it can be helpful to team up with others who are studying for the same test. Your actual studying should be done in as isolated an environment as possible, but the work of organizing the information and setting up the study plan can be divided up. In between study sessions, you can discuss with your teammates the concepts that you're all studying and quiz each other on the details. Just be sure that your teammates are as serious about the test as you are. If you find that your study time is being replaced with social time, you might need to find a new team.

Secret Key #2 – Make Your Studying Count

You're devoting a lot of time and effort to preparing for this test, so you want to be absolutely certain it will pay off. This means doing more than just reading the content and hoping you can remember it on test day. It's important to make every minute of study count. There are two main areas you can focus on to make your studying count:

Retention

It doesn't matter how much time you study if you can't remember the material. You need to make sure you are retaining the concepts. To check your retention of the information you're learning, try recalling it at later times with minimal prompting. Try carrying around flashcards and glance at one or two from time to time or ask a friend who's also studying for the test to quiz you.

To enhance your retention, look for ways to put the information into practice so that you can apply it rather than simply recalling it. If you're using the information in practical ways, it will be much easier to remember. Similarly, it helps to solidify a concept in your mind if you're not only reading it to yourself but also explaining it to someone else. Ask a friend to let you teach them about a concept you're a little shaky on (or speak aloud to an imaginary audience if necessary). As you try to summarize, define, give examples, and answer your friend's questions, you'll understand the concepts better and they will stay with you longer. Finally, step back for a big picture view and ask yourself how each piece of information fits with the whole subject. When you link the different concepts together and see them working together as a whole, it's easier to remember the individual components.

Finally, practice showing your work on any multi-step problems, even if you're just studying. Writing out each step you take to solve a problem will help solidify the process in your mind, and you'll be more likely to remember it during the test.

Modality

Modality simply refers to the means or method by which you study. Choosing a study modality that fits your own individual learning style is crucial. No two people learn best in exactly the same way, so it's important to know your strengths and use them to your advantage.

For example, if you learn best by visualization, focus on visualizing a concept in your mind and draw an image or a diagram. Try color-coding your notes, illustrating them, or creating symbols that will trigger your mind to recall a learned concept. If you learn best by hearing or discussing information, find a study partner who learns the same way or read aloud to yourself. Think about how to put the information in your own words. Imagine that you are giving a lecture on the topic and record yourself so you can listen to it later.

For any learning style, flashcards can be helpful. Organize the information so you can take advantage of spare moments to review. Underline key words or phrases. Use different colors for different categories. Mnemonic devices (such as creating a short list in which every item starts with the same letter) can also help with retention. Find what works best for you and use it to store the information in your mind most effectively and easily.

Secret Key #3 – Practice the Right Way

Your success on test day depends not only on how many hours you put into preparing, but also on whether you prepared the right way. It's good to check along the way to see if your studying is paying off. One of the most effective ways to do this is by taking practice tests to evaluate your progress. Practice tests are useful because they show exactly where you need to improve. Every time you take a practice test, pay special attention to these three groups of questions:

- The questions you got wrong
- The questions you had to guess on, even if you guessed right
- The questions you found difficult or slow to work through

This will show you exactly what your weak areas are, and where you need to devote more study time. Ask yourself why each of these questions gave you trouble. Was it because you didn't understand the material? Was it because you didn't remember the vocabulary? Do you need more repetitions on this type of question to build speed and confidence? Dig into those questions and figure out how you can strengthen your weak areas as you go back to review the material.

Additionally, many practice tests have a section explaining the answer choices. It can be tempting to read the explanation and think that you now have a good understanding of the concept. However, an explanation likely only covers part of the question's broader context. Even if the explanation makes sense, **go back and investigate** every concept related to the question until you're positive you have a thorough understanding.

As you go along, keep in mind that the practice test is just that: practice. Memorizing these questions and answers will not be very helpful on the actual test because it is unlikely to have any of the same exact questions. If you only know the right answers to the sample questions, you won't be prepared for the real thing. **Study the concepts** until you understand them fully, and then you'll be able to answer any question that shows up on the test.

It's important to wait on the practice tests until you're ready. If you take a test on your first day of study, you may be overwhelmed by the amount of material covered and how much you need to learn. Work up to it gradually.

On test day, you'll need to be prepared for answering questions, managing your time, and using the test-taking strategies you've learned. It's a lot to balance, like a mental marathon that will have a big impact on your future. Like training for a marathon, you'll need to start slowly and work your way up. When test day arrives, you'll be ready.

Start with the strategies you've read in the first two Secret Keys—plan your course and study in the way that works best for you. If you have time, consider using multiple study resources to get different approaches to the same concepts. It can be helpful to see difficult concepts from more than one angle. Then find a good source for practice tests. Many times, the test website will suggest potential study resources or provide sample tests.

Practice Test Strategy

When you're ready to start taking practice tests, follow this strategy:

1. Take the first test with no time constraints and with your notes and study guide handy. Take your time and focus on applying the strategies you've learned.
2. Take the second practice test open-book as well, but set a timer and practice pacing yourself to finish in time.
3. Take any other practice tests as if it were test day. Set a timer and put away your study materials. Sit at a table or desk in a quiet room, imagine yourself at the testing center, and answer questions as quickly and accurately as possible.
4. Keep repeating step 3 on a regular basis until you run out of practice tests or it's time for the actual test. Your mind will be ready for the schedule and stress of test day, and you'll be able to focus on recalling the material you've learned.

Secret Key #4 – Pace Yourself

Once you're fully prepared for the material on the test, your biggest challenge on test day will be managing your time. Just knowing that the clock is ticking can make you panic even if you have plenty of time left. Work on pacing yourself so you can build confidence against the time constraints of the exam. Pacing is a difficult skill to master, especially in a high-pressure environment, so **practice is vital**.

Set time expectations for your pace based on how much time is available. For example, if a section has 60 questions and the time limit is 30 minutes, you know you have to average 30 seconds or less per question in order to answer them all. Although 30 seconds is the hard limit, set 25 seconds per question as your goal, so you reserve extra time to spend on harder questions. When you budget extra time for the harder questions, you no longer have any reason to stress when those questions take longer to answer.

Don't let this time expectation distract you from working through the test at a calm, steady pace, but keep it in mind so you don't spend too much time on any one question. Recognize that taking extra time on one question you don't understand may keep you from answering two that you do understand later in the test. If your time limit for a question is up and you're still not sure of the answer, mark it and move on, and come back to it later if the time and the test format allow. If the testing format doesn't allow you to return to earlier questions, just make an educated guess; then put it out of your mind and move on.

On the easier questions, be careful not to rush. It may seem wise to hurry through them so you have more time for the challenging ones, but it's not worth missing one if you know the concept and just didn't take the time to read the question fully. Work efficiently but make sure you understand the question and have looked at all of the answer choices, since more than one may seem right at first.

Even if you're paying attention to the time, you may find yourself a little behind at some point. You should speed up to get back on track, but do so wisely. Don't panic; just take a few seconds less on each question until you're caught up. Don't guess without thinking, but do look through the answer choices and eliminate any you know are wrong. If you can get down to two choices, it is often worthwhile to guess from those. Once you've chosen an answer, move on and don't dwell on any that you skipped or had to hurry through. If a question was taking too long, chances are it was one of the harder ones, so you weren't as likely to get it right anyway.

On the other hand, if you find yourself getting ahead of schedule, it may be beneficial to slow down a little. The more quickly you work, the more likely you are to make a careless mistake that will affect your score. You've budgeted time for each question, so don't be afraid to spend that time. Practice an efficient but careful pace to get the most out of the time you have.

Secret Key #5 – Have a Plan for Guessing

When you're taking the test, you may find yourself stuck on a question. Some of the answer choices seem better than others, but you don't see the one answer choice that is obviously correct. What do you do?

The scenario described above is very common, yet most test takers have not effectively prepared for it. Developing and practicing a plan for guessing may be one of the single most effective uses of your time as you get ready for the exam.

In developing your plan for guessing, there are three questions to address:

- When should you start the guessing process?
- How should you narrow down the choices?
- Which answer should you choose?

When to Start the Guessing Process

Unless your plan for guessing is to select C every time (which, despite its merits, is not what we recommend), you need to leave yourself enough time to apply your answer elimination strategies. Since you have a limited amount of time for each question, that means that if you're going to give yourself the best shot at guessing correctly, you have to decide quickly whether or not you will guess.

Of course, the best-case scenario is that you don't have to guess at all, so first, see if you can answer the question based on your knowledge of the subject and basic reasoning skills. Focus on the key words in the question and try to jog your memory of related topics. Give yourself a chance to bring the knowledge to mind, but once you realize that you don't have (or you can't access) the knowledge you need to answer the question, it's time to start the guessing process.

It's almost always better to start the guessing process too early than too late. It only takes a few seconds to remember something and answer the question from knowledge. Carefully eliminating wrong answer choices takes longer. Plus, going through the process of eliminating answer choices can actually help jog your memory.

Summary: Start the guessing process as soon as you decide that you can't answer the question based on your knowledge.

How to Narrow Down the Choices

The next chapter in this book (**Test-Taking Strategies**) includes a wide range of strategies for how to approach questions and how to look for answer choices to eliminate. You will definitely want to read those carefully, practice them, and figure out which ones work best for you. Here though, we're going to address a mindset rather than a particular strategy.

Your chances of guessing an answer correctly depend on how many options you are choosing from.

How many choices you have	How likely you are to guess correctly
5	20%
4	25%
3	33%
2	50%
1	100%

You can see from this chart just how valuable it is to be able to eliminate incorrect answers and make an educated guess, but there are two things that many test takers do that cause them to miss out on the benefits of guessing:

- Accidentally eliminating the correct answer
- Selecting an answer based on an impression

We'll look at the first one here, and the second one in the next section.

To avoid accidentally eliminating the correct answer, we recommend a thought exercise called **the $5 challenge**. In this challenge, you only eliminate an answer choice from contention if you are willing to bet $5 on it being wrong. Why $5? Five dollars is a small but not insignificant amount of money. It's an amount you could afford to lose but wouldn't want to throw away. And while losing $5 once might not hurt too much, doing it twenty times will set you back $100. In the same way, each small decision you make—eliminating a choice here, guessing on a question there—won't by itself impact your score very much, but when you put them all together, they can make a big difference. By holding each answer choice elimination decision to a higher standard, you can reduce the risk of accidentally eliminating the correct answer.

The $5 challenge can also be applied in a positive sense: If you are willing to bet $5 that an answer choice *is* correct, go ahead and mark it as correct.

Summary: Only eliminate an answer choice if you are willing to bet $5 that it is wrong.

Which Answer to Choose

You're taking the test. You've run into a hard question and decided you'll have to guess. You've eliminated all the answer choices you're willing to bet $5 on. Now you have to pick an answer. Why do we even need to talk about this? Why can't you just pick whichever one you feel like when the time comes?

The answer to these questions is that if you don't come into the test with a plan, you'll rely on your impression to select an answer choice, and if you do that, you risk falling into a trap. The test writers know that everyone who takes their test will be guessing on some of the questions, so they intentionally write wrong answer choices to seem plausible. You still have to pick an answer though, and if the wrong answer choices are designed to look right, how can you ever be sure that you're not falling for their trap? The best solution we've found to this dilemma is to take the decision out of your hands entirely. Here is the process we recommend:

Once you've eliminated any choices that you are confident (willing to bet $5) are wrong, select the first remaining choice as your answer.

Whether you choose to select the first remaining choice, the second, or the last, the important thing is that you use some preselected standard. Using this approach guarantees that you will not be enticed into selecting an answer choice that looks right, because you are not basing your decision on how the answer choices look.

This is not meant to make you question your knowledge. Instead, it is to help you recognize the difference between your knowledge and your impressions. There's a huge difference between thinking an answer is right because of what you know, and thinking an answer is right because it looks or sounds like it should be right.

Summary: To ensure that your selection is appropriately random, make a predetermined selection from among all answer choices you have not eliminated.

Test-Taking Strategies

This section contains a list of test-taking strategies that you may find helpful as you work through the test. By taking what you know and applying logical thought, you can maximize your chances of answering any question correctly!

It is very important to realize that every question is different and every person is different: no single strategy will work on every question, and no single strategy will work for every person. That's why we've included all of them here, so you can try them out and determine which ones work best for different types of questions and which ones work best for you.

Question Strategies

Read Carefully

Read the question and answer choices carefully. Don't miss the question because you misread the terms. You have plenty of time to read each question thoroughly and make sure you understand what is being asked. Yet a happy medium must be attained, so don't waste too much time. You must read carefully, but efficiently.

Contextual Clues

Look for contextual clues. If the question includes a word you are not familiar with, look at the immediate context for some indication of what the word might mean. Contextual clues can often give you all the information you need to decipher the meaning of an unfamiliar word. Even if you can't determine the meaning, you may be able to narrow down the possibilities enough to make a solid guess at the answer to the question.

Prefixes

If you're having trouble with a word in the question or answer choices, try dissecting it. Take advantage of every clue that the word might include. Prefixes and suffixes can be a huge help. Usually they allow you to determine a basic meaning. Pre- means before, post- means after, pro - is positive, de- is negative. From prefixes and suffixes, you can get an idea of the general meaning of the word and try to put it into context.

Hedge Words

Watch out for critical hedge words, such as *likely*, *may*, *can*, *sometimes*, *often*, *almost*, *mostly*, *usually*, *generally*, *rarely*, and *sometimes*. Question writers insert these hedge phrases to cover every possibility. Often an answer choice will be wrong simply because it leaves no room for exception. Be on guard for answer choices that have definitive words such as *exactly* and *always*.

Switchback Words

Stay alert for *switchbacks*. These are the words and phrases frequently used to alert you to shifts in thought. The most common switchback words are *but*, *although*, and *however*. Others include *nevertheless*, *on the other hand*, *even though*, *while*, *in spite of*, *despite*, *regardless of*. Switchback words are important to catch because they can change the direction of the question or an answer choice.

Face Value

When in doubt, use common sense. Accept the situation in the problem at face value. Don't read too much into it. These problems will not require you to make wild assumptions. If you have to go beyond creativity and warp time or space in order to have an answer choice fit the question, then you should move on and consider the other answer choices. These are normal problems rooted in reality. The applicable relationship or explanation may not be readily apparent, but it is there for you to figure out. Use your common sense to interpret anything that isn't clear.

Answer Choice Strategies

Answer Selection

The most thorough way to pick an answer choice is to identify and eliminate wrong answers until only one is left, then confirm it is the correct answer. Sometimes an answer choice may immediately seem right, but be careful. The test writers will usually put more than one reasonable answer choice on each question, so take a second to read all of them and make sure that the other choices are not equally obvious. As long as you have time left, it is better to read every answer choice than to pick the first one that looks right without checking the others.

Answer Choice Families

An answer choice family consists of two (in rare cases, three) answer choices that are very similar in construction and cannot all be true at the same time. If you see two answer choices that are direct opposites or parallels, one of them is usually the correct answer. For instance, if one answer choice says that quantity x increases and another either says that quantity x decreases (opposite) or says that quantity y increases (parallel), then those answer choices would fall into the same family. An answer choice that doesn't match the construction of the answer choice family is more likely to be incorrect. Most questions will not have answer choice families, but when they do appear, you should be prepared to recognize them.

Eliminate Answers

Eliminate answer choices as soon as you realize they are wrong, but make sure you consider all possibilities. If you are eliminating answer choices and realize that the last one you are left with is also wrong, don't panic. Start over and consider each choice again. There may be something you missed the first time that you will realize on the second pass.

Avoid Fact Traps

Don't be distracted by an answer choice that is factually true but doesn't answer the question. You are looking for the choice that answers the question. Stay focused on what the question is asking for so you don't accidentally pick an answer that is true but incorrect. Always go back to the question and make sure the answer choice you've selected actually answers the question and is not merely a true statement.

Extreme Statements

In general, you should avoid answers that put forth extreme actions as standard practice or proclaim controversial ideas as established fact. An answer choice that states the "process should be used in certain situations, if…" is much more likely to be correct than one that states the "process should be discontinued completely." The first is a calm rational statement and doesn't even make a definitive, uncompromising stance, using a hedge word *if* to provide wiggle room, whereas the second choice is a radical idea and far more extreme.

Benchmark

As you read through the answer choices and you come across one that seems to answer the question well, mentally select that answer choice. This is not your final answer, but it's the one that will help you evaluate the other answer choices. The one that you selected is your benchmark or standard for judging each of the other answer choices. Every other answer choice must be compared to your benchmark. That choice is correct until proven otherwise by another answer choice beating it. If you find a better answer, then that one becomes your new benchmark. Once you've decided that no other choice answers the question as well as your benchmark, you have your final answer.

Predict the Answer

Before you even start looking at the answer choices, it is often best to try to predict the answer. When you come up with the answer on your own, it is easier to avoid distractions and traps because you will know exactly what to look for. The right answer choice is unlikely to be word-for-word what you came up with, but it should be a close match. Even if you are confident that you have the right answer, you should still take the time to read each option before moving on.

General Strategies

Tough Questions

If you are stumped on a problem or it appears too hard or too difficult, don't waste time. Move on! Remember though, if you can quickly check for obviously incorrect answer choices, your chances of guessing correctly are greatly improved. Before you completely give up, at least try to knock out a couple of possible answers. Eliminate what you can and then guess at the remaining answer choices before moving on.

Check Your Work

Since you will probably not know every term listed and the answer to every question, it is important that you get credit for the ones that you do know. Don't miss any questions through careless mistakes. If at all possible, try to take a second to look back over your answer selection and make sure you've selected the correct answer choice and haven't made a costly careless mistake (such as marking an answer choice that you didn't mean to mark). This quick double check should more than pay for itself in caught mistakes for the time it costs.

Pace Yourself

It's easy to be overwhelmed when you're looking at a page full of questions; your mind is confused and full of random thoughts, and the clock is ticking down faster than you would like. Calm down and maintain the pace that you have set for yourself. Especially as you get down to the last few minutes of the test, don't let the small numbers on the clock make you panic. As long as you are on track by monitoring your pace, you are guaranteed to have time for each question.

Don't Rush

It is very easy to make errors when you are in a hurry. Maintaining a fast pace in answering questions is pointless if it makes you miss questions that you would have gotten right otherwise. Test writers like to include distracting information and wrong answers that seem right. Taking a little extra time to avoid careless mistakes can make all the difference in your test score. Find a pace that allows you to be confident in the answers that you select.

Keep Moving

Panicking will not help you pass the test, so do your best to stay calm and keep moving. Taking deep breaths and going through the answer elimination steps you practiced can help to break through a stress barrier and keep your pace.

Final Notes

The combination of a solid foundation of content knowledge and the confidence that comes from practicing your plan for applying that knowledge is the key to maximizing your performance on test day. As your foundation of content knowledge is built up and strengthened, you'll find that the strategies included in this chapter become more and more effective in helping you quickly sift through the distractions and traps of the test to isolate the correct answer.

Now it's time to move on to the test content chapters of this book, but be sure to keep your goal in mind. As you read, think about how you will be able to apply this information on the test. If you've already seen sample questions for the test and you have an idea of the question format and style, try to come up with questions of your own that you can answer based on what you're reading. This will give you valuable practice applying your knowledge in the same ways you can expect to on test day.

Good luck and good studying!

Scientific Concepts

Infection Control

Sanitization procedures

Sanitization is part of the daily rituals performed. Salons do need to not use sterilization methods to clean tools and surfaces. This is used only for surgical procedures.

Surfaces that require sanitization are floors, windows, screens, curtains, rest rooms, doorknobs, and the outside of all containers. Floors should receive a thorough sweeping after each client. Floors should be mopped and vacuumed daily. Garbage must be stored in a metal can with a self-closing lid. The trash must be emptied as needed throughout the work day. Dust and nail filings must be controlled by proper disinfection methods that will kill any pathogens or living microorganisms. Hot and cold running water should be readily available. Wash hands after and before servicing each client. Hands should be washed before touching the face or the eyes. Hands should be washed before eating. Hands should be washed before and after using the bathroom facilities.

Sanitization supplies and restrictions

Supplies that should be on hand for decontamination purposes are disinfectants, sanitizing soap, hot and cold running water, drinking cups, trash bags, broom, dustpan, mop, bucket, toilet tissue, paper towels, liquid hand soap, and freshly laundered or disposable towels for each client. Additionally:

- Food products and salon products should not be contained in the same refrigerator.
- Pets or animals should not be permitted, except for trained, Seeing Eye dogs.
- A complete list of each state's rules and regulations are available at the State Board of Cosmetology or Health Department.
- Disinfectants should be used in conjunction with the manufacturer's directions. Failure to do so may cause potential dangers to self and clients.
- Hand washing procedures should be followed explicitly.
- Rodents or insects should not be tolerated on the premises.
- Cooking areas must be separate from the salon.
- Living quarters should not be part of the salon.

Disinfectants

Surfaces that require thorough cleaning and disinfection periodically throughout the day include: tables, counter tops, mirrors, telephone receivers, door knobs, and bathroom surfaces. It is suggested to have one set of disinfected implements available while a second set is being disinfected. The tools or implements required are clippers, nippers, cuticle pushers, scissors, reusable forms, manicure and pedicure bowls. Each of these must be disinfected after service of each client. Manufacturers have included disinfection recommendations on the files and buffers produced that can be disinfected. You should not try to disinfect porous buffers, files, drill bits and wooden sticks as the tendency to absorb water makes it impossible. Do not try to disinfect files contaminated with blood. Brushes used in the application of acrylics and gels are not subject to disinfection techniques.

Quaternary ammonium compounds

Quaternary ammonium compounds, (quats), are different agents blended together to result in a safe and fast-acting cleansing solution. Quats are the most cost effective of the disinfectants used. Gloves and masks should be used whenever cleaning with disinfectants. Quats are useful for disinfecting table and counter tops. Implements or tools should be submersed for a period of ten minutes to be most effective. A 1:1000 solution of quats requires a one to five minute immersion time. Longer periods of immersion are not recommended for metal objects as there may be a possible danger of erosion. Some quats are formulated to lessen the corrosion and rust effects. Decontamination of surfaces should be washed first with a detergent, followed by a disinfectant. This procedure should be repeated. Leave the last application on the surface and allow to air dry.

Alcohol and bleach

Alcohol should be used to immerse the implements for a period of ten to twenty minutes. Caution should be used with alcohol as it is extremely flammable. Alcohol is slower and less effective than other disinfectants. Alcohol is not effective as a wipe on and wipe off solution. Alcohol tends to evaporate quickly. Dilution should be above 70% and less than 80% to ensure the highest rate of effectiveness. Alcohol needs water to work as it requires hydration. Alcohol can corrode sharp implements. Bleach can be used as a disinfectant to immerse an implement for a period of ten to twenty minutes. Bleach should be used with caution as it can damage skin and eyes and discolor clothing. The State Board of Cosmetology or Health Department can provide information on the individual states time requirements or ban on these solutions.

Phenolics

Phenolics are not to be used on rubber or plastic surfaces as these materials are not compatible with this solution. Use may lead to softening or destruction of such materials. Gloves should be worn when using the concentrated liquid to prevent harm to the skin and eyes. It is advisable to use a controlled spraying technique when applying the phenolic to surfaces. Wear a mask to reduce agitation to the lining of the nose, throat, and lungs caused by spraying the fine mist. Leave the phenolic to sit for about five to ten minutes while the mist dies down. Examine state regulations for proper disposal methods due to the high alkaline pH values. Phenolic solutions should be prepared and used according to the manufacturer's guidelines. Phenolics provide a good level of effective protection. However, phenolics can be more costly than other available disinfectants.

Sanitation procedures for implements

Sanitation of metal implements is required. One recommendation that can be an added benefit is the use of two sets. One set can be sanitized while another is in use. The sanitation process requires a minimum of twenty minutes. Soap and warm water should be used to wash all implements. Washing should be followed by a complete rinse of all soap particles. Then, dry implements thoroughly with a laundered towel or a disposable towel. Immerse implements in disinfectant and follow the manufacturer's directives for disinfection procedures and time frames. Removal of the implements from the disinfectant requires a thorough rinsing, followed by a thorough drying of implements with a clean or disposable towel. State regulations should be followed for storage of sanitized implements to prevent contamination while in storage. Some regulations provide storage in sealed containers, sealed plastic bags, or in cabinet sanitizers.

Storage of clean implements

Implements that have been through the decontamination process should be stored in Ultraviolet (U.V.) sanitizers. This allows them to stay clean. Salon sanitizers are not of the quality to sanitize the implements. Implements must go through the decontamination process and the solutions should be used accordingly before storage in U.V. sanitizers. Viruses are not controlled by the use of the Ultraviolet sanitizer. The Ultraviolet rays cannot decontaminate the crevices of the implements or tools stored. If an Ultraviolet sanitizer is not available, it is acceptable to use an airtight container to store decontaminated implements. It is important to follow proper storage procedures to keep implements free from containments. Bead sterilizers are devices that would only be effective if it could heat to 325 degrees for at least 30 minutes, which it cannot. FDA regulations are not advisable as proof of effective sterilization capabilities.

Toxic chemicals

Formalin is a disinfectant that contains an unsafe amount of formaldehyde. Formaldehyde has been researched and found to be a cancer causing agent. It is advisable to avoid contact, especially as it is a poison that can be absorbed through inhalation or touch. Formaldehyde can cause extreme irritation to the eyes, nose, throat, and lungs. Symptoms associated with rashes, irritations, and dryness may be due to contact with this chemical. Formaldehyde, a known allergic sensitizer, has been associated with allergic reactions that are similar to attacks of chronic bronchitis or asthma. Prolonged exposure or repeated contact with formaldehyde may produce these symptoms. These symptoms tend to flare up after a few months and increase with time. Formalin's use is illegal in some states. However, there was a time that formalin was used as a disinfectant and as a dry cabinet sanitizer.

Clean up of blood spills

OSHA requires that all blood spills be mandatorily reported to the employer by the employee. Additional mandates required by the State Cosmetology Board may include the use of a tuberculocidal disinfectant to clean up any blood that is visible to the eye. Blood spills should never be cleaned without the use of gloves and safety precautions. Tuberculocidal disinfectants are formulated with a phenolic base. One that has an EPA registered, hospital-level is far superior to the normal salon quality disinfectant. However, the tuberculocidal disinfectant should be used following the precautions that would be used with any phenolic based disinfectant. Contrary to the name, the tuberculocidal disinfectants will not be effective in the prevention of tuberculosis. Tuberculosis is just one of several pathogens that can cause disease or illness that are found in blood.

Overexposure and allergic contact dermatitis

A nail technician must use caution to avoid contact with the skin of any nail enhancement product. This is essential because nail technicians can have a sensitivity built up due to their overexposure of a product. These are the particular areas that they are most susceptible to dermatitis: between the thumb and pointer finger; on the wrist or palm; the facial cheeks; and on the cuticles, finger tips or tissues of the nail bed. Nail technicians should avoid smoothing wet brushes with their fingertips to reduce the advent of red, inflamed fingertips. Arms should not be placed on towels where nail enhancement products may be present. Wipe down containers that may have excess amounts of monomer traces on the outside to prevent contact with the palms of the hands. Exposure to the face and cheeks should be avoided.

Avoid using an excess of liquid monomer and do not use the liquid monomer to smooth the enhancement surface. Monomer should not be used to clean up the edges, under the nail, or sidewalls. Always avoid skin contact with monomer, U.V. gels, or adhesives as this can damage the skin. Always wear gloves and avoid touching the ends of the brush with your fingertips. Avoid creating a special blend as you may produce a chemical imbalance within the products. Read and follow the directions to avoid unnecessary mistakes. An allergic reaction should be promptly noted and all products with that chemical should be stopped immediately. Extended and habitual contact from the chemical is the reason for the allergic reaction, not medications or illnesses. Products and residues from all products should be cleaned from the work area regularly.

Irritant contact dermatitis

Irritant contact dermatitis can be caused by corrosive chemicals irritating or damaging the skin. The immune system attempts to dilute the irritant by flooding the area with water. This produces swelling in the area. The blood releases a chemical known as histamines which enlarge the vessels around the injury or swollen area. This further helps in the removal of irritants. Histamines are the reason that the area is scratchy and sore. The tap water present in the salon is an irritant which produces sore, cracked, chapped hands. The nail technician should be careful to dry hands and moisturize with hand creams. This will help in reducing the loss of skin oils produced from overexposure to hand washing. One should note a particularly area to try to pinpoint unexplained irritations. In this way, you can avoid the irritant that caused the skin problem in the future.

Susceptibility to disease

A person with poor dietary habits can have a reduced ability to fight off disease or infection. Adequate, healthy nutrition provides a person with antibodies and maintains higher levels of energy. These levels are required when a person is sick and trying to fight off infection. This is one reason why the young and the old are usually at the most risk from disease. Persons that do a great deal of travel may find their exposure to risk increased. Some of these exposures may be to diseases that the person has no natural immunity. Likewise, some of these diseases may have long incubation periods. Persons can be carriers of these diseases and have no outward symptoms. Health care workers, service workers, and persons who deal directly with the public have an increase in exposure to disease, as well.

Immunity

Immunity can be described as the bodies' ability to fight against disease or infection. A person with a natural immunity fights infection off in three ways. Our protective, unbroken skin and its mantle provide one way. Our bodies have natural secretions, digestive juices, and perspirations designed to prevent the growth of pathogens which cause infection and disease. Our blood stream is specifically designed white blood cells that kill pathogens that may find their way into our blood. Once a body has effectively fought off a disease, antibodies stay in the bloodstream. A naturally acquired immunity occurs when antibodies prevent the reoccurrence of the disease. However, an artificial acquired immunity can be obtained through serums or vaccines. The vaccine is a small sampling of the disease introduced into the blood stream. The immune system reacts by producing antibodies that help fight off the disease.

Spread of infections

Dirty implements can be used to spread bacteria and other harmful pathogens. Bacteria can spread at alarming rates. Nail files, cuticle nippers, manicuring tables, trash cans, and towels can be breeding grounds for bacteria and other harmful pathogens. Parasites can live in and on your customer's nails, hands, and feet. The risk of this parasite to you and your salon is increased at the time of service. When an artificial nail is applied to an infected natural nail, the infection can be trapped between the artificial and the natural nail. Cold symptoms like coughing and sneezing can cause bacteria to spread in the salon. A source of contamination can be found in an open sore or wound. Every surface in the salon can be a potential breeding ground for pathogens to grow. Bathrooms are an ideal place for germs to grow.

Reducing risk of infection

Proper sanitation and disinfection procedures should be followed stringently. Clients are concerned about their environment and health care needs. Sharing your knowledge concerning sanitation and disinfection of your salon can ease some of their concerns. Clients with severe colds, influenza, chicken pox, and other contagious disease can cause a health threat. A client that is sick or contagious should not be given beauty treatments and should be advised to seek medical assistance. You should not work if you are contagious. Clients that have an open would need to be seen by a physician. A written release from the physician is advisable upon their return for services. Careful attention to the skin and cuticles should be given to avoid overfilling, bruising, or wounds. The professional will eat properly, obtain adequate rest, and protect themselves with proper hygiene.

Safely handling blood

Procedures used whenever blood is a consideration are to be strictly followed. First, it is essential that you put gloves on right away. Tell your client about the blood and apologize. Then, using cotton and an antiseptic apply a slight pressure to the injury. If the blood flow is still evident, then apply alum or styptic powder with a cotton-wrapped orangewood stick. Discard the stick after use. Styptic pens are not recommended due to their unsanitary nature. Finish the manicure, if permissible. Proper disposal of the blood contaminated materials and implements should be strictly adhered. Disinfection of all contaminated implements is advised with an approved disinfectant. Don't forget to thoroughly cleanse hands with antibacterial soap. Universal precautions are required when handling blood and/or bodily fluids to ensure your safety and that of your clients.

SDS

The information provided on a safety data sheet (SDS, formerly MSDS) is available to everyone that may come in contact with a chemical. The United States regulates this availability through OSHA. The document must be located on property's that offer exposure to the chemical being used. These documents must be filed on site in an easy to locate, open view at all times. The format of the document has sixteen sections including identification of chemicals with potentially hazardous ingredients listed, physical hazards that may be possible, health hazards that may be possible, primary routes that the chemical takes to gain entry into the body, the permissible exposure limitations of the product, carcinogen hazards, handling precautionary measures, control and protection procedures, emergency and first aid contact information and procedures, storage and disposal procedures.

The SDS may have emergency phone numbers listing a poison control center that has been provided known to have specific information related to the chemical in question. Hazard ranking: 0-least hazardous; 1-slightly hazardous; 2-moderately hazardous; 3-highly hazardous; 4-extremely hazardous. Extinguishers are rated as follows: A-trash, wood, paper, and plastic; B-grease, liquids, alcohol, and acetone; and C-electrical. A multipurpose extinguisher will have the rating of ABC.

The product's specific gravity may be listed. Specific gravity refers to the how the water reacts to water. If water is thrown on some substances, and the gravity weight is less than the water, then it is expected that the substance will float to the top of the water. Some explosive conditions can result as the fire spreads in conjunction with the amount of water used to put out the fire.

Procedures and precautionary measures

The SDS has information on how to safely handle the product in normal use. The procedures are given on how to properly handle any clean up or spills that may occur during the products use. The protective measures are given to ensure the well being and safety of those persons who may come into contact with the chemical. Additionally, the requirements for ventilations, skin protection, and eye protection will be described. In the event of an accident, the document's information is to be used to respond to the emergency using the safety recommendations prescribed. The treatment of potentially harmful exposures will be listed, along with advice for first aid care and emergency phone numbers. Storage of the chemical should be followed, along with proper and safe disposal techniques.

Hazards and exposure

The SDS provides specific information regarding the possible hazards that the individual ingredients of the product may present. These hazards can create physical situations that could cause cataclysmic harm to people. Such cataclysmic harm may be in the chemicals reaction that could result in an explosion, fire, or the release of the chemical into the air. The product's chemicals may present medical conditions that bring harmful results to the individual. Overexposure and swallowing hazards are ways that these chemicals can harm an individual. The short and long term effects associated with overexposure of the chemical must be listed in detail. The chemical's potential entrance through the skin, mouth, or lungs must be listed, along with cancer causing agents that may measures over a $1/10^{th}$ percentile in the product.

Common chemicals and hazards

A nail technician may use nail polish, nail polish removers, acrylic nail liquids, acrylic nail powders, acrylic nail primers, dehydrators, light cured gel nail supplies, no light gels, no light activators, cuticle oils, cuticle creams, fabric wrap adhesives, and a variety of other nail care products. Manufacturers provide instructions on how to use these products safely. This information is found in the safety data sheets (SDS) provided by the manufacturer as regulated by the United States government. Additionally, there are some harmful effects that can be produced by overexposure or misuse of a product. Overexposure has early warning signals that should trigger you to take action. Some of these early warning signs include: rash, skin irritations, lightheadedness, insomnia, runny nose, sore, dry throat, watery eyes, tingling toes, fatigue, irritability, sluggishness, and breathing irregularities.

Safe working environment

The salon should have proper ventilation that has an existing exhaust system to the outside. The salon should not store food and beauty products in the same refrigerators. A separate refrigerator should be used for each purpose. Safety Data Sheets should be on display and within easy reach of existing personnel in need of safety or product information. The workstation should be clean and sanitary. Implements should be stored in sanitary, closed containers or Ultraviolet storage compartments. Plastic disposable bags should be in containers that close. Bathrooms should have supplies and be clean and sanitary. Safety equipment should be worn by existing personnel. Aerosol cans are not used; instead products are applied with safer pumps or brush on methods.

Emergency numbers are posted in a visible area. Salon workers should be advised of emergency procedures.

Skin Anatomy & Physiology

Functions of skin

The eight specific functions of the skin are protection, prevention of loss fluids, external stimulus impulses, heat regulation, secretion, excretion, absorption, and respiration. The outside covering of the skin is a protective barrier. This barrier protects the body from injury. This barrier also protects the body from attacking bacteria that may cause infection or disease. The skin keeps the blood and body fluids contained within the body. External stimulus impulses are reactions to heat, cold, touch, pressure, and pain. Nerve endings in the skin give off a sensitive reactive impulse used to signal the body to an action. This is used to protect the body against injury. One example occurs when a person touches something hot and jerks their hand away.

The skin controls the temperature regulation functions. The body keeps its temperature regulated at an internal temperature of 98.6 degrees Fahrenheit. When the body is exposed to hot or cold environments the blood and sweat glands work to either warm or cool the body to help maintain this temperature. Secretion of the oil is produced from the sebaceous glands. This oil is called sebum. Sebum is the fatty, oil useful for maintaining the moisture levels within the skin. Sebum allows the skin to slow down moisture evaporation. It also aids in resisting skin penetration of an excess of water. Salt and waste chemicals are eliminated from the body by the process of excretion. During perspiration sweat (sudoriferous) glands work to eliminate these chemicals out from the body. Perspiration occurs as the body sweats through pores in the skin.

The function of the skin called absorption occurs when the pores take in small amounts of chemicals, drugs, or cosmetics. Absorption can cause damage to the skin when contact with the substance absorbed is harmful to the person. This may be due to the toxicity of the contact or the person's allergic reactions. Caution should be used when applying any chemical that may harm the person through this process. This awareness will assist the nail technician in making appropriate choices for skin care. Respiration is the process that allows the skin to breathe. The skin can breathe through its pores. Absorption may cause a reduction in this process. Respiration has two phases involving the skin. The first phase involves the absorption of oxygen through the pores. The second phase allows the elimination of eliminates carbon dioxide out of the pores.

Disorders

The golden rule is the standard that you use to determine whether a client should receive a nail care treatment. This standard should prevent infections from disease and bacteria from spreading onto surfaces in the salon or to other people. Red, sore, or swollen skin indicates a condition of inflammation. Skin that has obvious signs of pus pockets is infected. A torn or cut epidermis exposes the layer of skin is known as broken skin. Symptoms of raised skin consist of lesions in various stages of disease. However, a diagnosis should never be made by the nail technician. Doctors are licensed to give diagnosis, and as such, should be the ones to give the diagnosis. Client with skin that has been infected, inflamed, broken, or raised is subject to denial of services. This denial should be given tactfully and gently.

Psoriasis

Psoriasis has mild to severe symptoms which include scaly plaques of skin. Some bleeding may be present in the severe cases. Psoriasis can cover the entire body or be localized. Psoriasis develops as silvery, scales on the skin. There are numerous types of this disease. The kind that affects the sole of the foot and the palm of the hand is called pustular psoriasis and psoriatic keratoderma. Other types that affect the hands and the feet are known as psoriasis of the nails, psoriatic arthritis, and interdigital psoriasis. The pustular type creates pus blisters. These blisters dry out as brown scabs which peel. The keratoderma variety is gray or yellowish, with deep, agonizing cracks and callus characteristics. The interdigital form or white variety creates white tissue between the fingers and toes. Many times, this form is wrongly mistaken as a fungal infection.

Calluses

Calluses are caused by a friction from an outside source. The friction rubs against the skin resulting in a callus. Callus appears as an enlarged, red spot on skin that has been irritated by the excessive rubbing. Many calluses appear on the ball of the foot. Stresses of external causes can produce a buildup of keratin in the form of a thick callus. Skin that does not create this keratin will normally form a blister instead. Gait abnormalities or walking irregularities may produce stresses on the foot that lead to the formation of calluses. Hands may have calluses from work or exterior stresses to the hand. The keratin that is used to form the callus has a yellowish color. Feet and hands with calluses may receive nail care treatments. However, the calluses should only be softened and smoothed, not detached.

Friction blisters

Friction blisters are the end result of injury that results from an external cause. The external cause may be from burns, chemical irritants, fungal infections, or other irritants. Pressure on one spot can cause a blister to develop on the skin. These are classified as bullas that are filled with a yellowish, tissue fluid. The fluid collects under the skin just beneath the stratum granulosum, or middle layer of the skin. Avoidance of rupture of the blister is advised. The blister usually will heal of its own accord. However, if the blister is ruptured a topical antibiotic ointment applied with a dressing is recommended. Nail care treatment should not be provided due to the risk of infection. Should an open blister develop an infection, it is advisable to seek medical care. The external cause of the blister should be avoided.

Warts

Warts are caused by viral infections. The virus called human papillomavirus (HPV), proliferate inside the nuclei of the cells to cause growth. Papillary growths appear as stretched out bulges in the form of a wart or papilloma. Warts are known as plantar wart verruca. Warts are actually non-cancerous, tumors of the skin. This is caused as the body protects itself. The protection is a growth, or barrier around the virus that is invading the skin. The invasion of the virus is the result of an injury, friction, nail biting, or scratching that has allowed a point of entry into the skin. Typically, the virus has a lengthy incubation period. It is believed that people are born with immunity to the virus as only 10% of the population ever gets a wart. Nail care treatment is recommended with use of sanitation procedures.

Integumentary system

The Integumentary system is described as the largest structure in the body. The skin, the oil and sweat glands, sensory receptors, hair, and nails are all part of this systems protective structure. The skin has two layers, the dermis and the epidermis. The layers provide protective covering over the body's internal organs. Likewise, the sensory receptors are responsible for the body's sense of touch. This system is also responsible for regulating the body's internal temperatures. This system is impacted when a person runs a fever. Other exposures to extreme heat or extreme cold temperatures may have a negative impact on this system, as well. A nail technician can have direct or indirect influence on this system. Nail treatment applications and nail care products should be applied in accordance with the manufacturer's directions to ensure safe applications.

Dermatitis and overexposure

Skin problems associated with the fingernail include dermatitis and overexposure. Dermatitis is an unusual skin inflammation that is caused by contact or allergens. In the case of contact dermatitis, the skin comes into contact or touches a substance that causes the skin to become inflamed. This inflammation may be of a short duration or last for a longer period of time. However, in the case of allergic contact dermatitis a substance has triggered an allergic reaction. The substance may have a particular ingredient present which has triggered the allergic reaction. Sometimes, these reactions are due to overexposure to the skin which creates increased sensitivity to the product. This sensitization in increased with every use of the product. Therefore, it is important to prevent contact with the skin. Free margin refers to the 1/16" protective gap between the product and the skin.

Nerves of the arm

The 4 key nerves of the arm are:

Musculocutaneous Nerve	Supplies all flexor muscles of the arm (which are in the anterior compartment). In the region between the biceps and brachialis muscles, it becomes the lateral cutaneous nerve of forearm - a nerve that supplies much of the forearm skin.
Radial Nerve	Supplies extensor muscles which are in the arm's posterior compartment. It descends inferolaterally alongside the deep brachial artery around the humerus in the radial groove, where it divides into a deep and superficial branch. The distribution of the deep branch is entirely muscular, which the superficial branch is solely cutaneous and supplies the dorsum of the hand and digits.
Median Nerve	Does not have branches in the arm. Initially, it runs on the lateral side of brachial artery, which it crosses at the middle of the arm. It descends to the cubital fossa beneath the bicipital aponeurosis.
Ulnar Nerve	Does not have branches in the arm. It passes anterior to the triceps muscle on the brachial artery's medial side. It passes posterior to the elbow's medial epicondyle and medial to the olecranon process to enter the forearm.

Receptors

The types of receptors are:

Mechanoreceptors	Sensitive to mechanical stimuli such as touch, pressure, stretch, hearing, position and movement, balance, vibration, and muscle contraction. Pressoreceptors and baroreceptors are also part of this group.
Thermoreceptors	Sensitive to changes in temperature, heat, or cold.
Photoreceptors	Sensitive to light and some are involved in vision.
Chemoreceptors	Sensitive to chemical stimuli such as oxygen, carbon dioxide, glucose, hormones, etc.
Nociceptors	Pain receptors that respond to noxious stimuli.

Cell growth and metabolism

Cell growth occurs when cells receive the right amount of food, oxygen, and water. Cells must eliminate waste and maintain the correct temperature to grow. If one of these elements is not present, then the cells' growth will be harmed. The bodies' cells do have the ability of repairing themselves during a life cycle. Reproduction of a cell occurs through a division process referred to as mitosis. Metabolism is a complex chemical method that allows the body cells to be fed and energized. Anabolism and catabolism are two phases of metabolism. Larger molecules are formed from smaller ones in the process of anabolism. This is essential in cell growth and repair. In releasing energy, catabolism is used to break down larger molecules into smaller ones. Homeostasis or internal stability is obtained when the body uses the energy we manufacture, otherwise weight may be gained.

Skeletal system

The skeletal system functions as the part of the body that makes up the bony structure. This bony structure is composed of 206 bones. These bones are notably the hardest tissue found in the body. The connective tissues of the bone consists of one-third animal matter, and two-thirds calcium carbonate and calcium phosphate substances. This bony structure permits the shape and support of the body. The skeletal system provides a protective covering over the internal organs and systems of the body. The bone serves as a supplement for muscles, acting as a lever to produce movement. The bony structure produces various blood cells in the formulation of the red bone marrow. The bone provides storage for minerals. These minerals are most commonly known as calcium, phosphorus, magnesium, and sodium. The study of bones, their composition and structure, and purpose is called osteology.

Blood

One of the most important functions of the blood is to provide water, oxygen, food, and secretions to all the cells found in the body. This nutrient rich fluid averages about 8-10 pints of blood per adult. Blood functions as a waste removal system. Blood is used to transport carbon dioxide and waste products through the lungs, skin, kidneys, and the large intestine for the purpose of elimination. Blood assists in regulating the body's temperature. This regulation feature is a necessary protection in times of exposure to heat and cold. The normal body temperature registers at 98.6 degrees. Additionally, blood provides a protective agent by using its white blood cells to act against and to prevent the spread of harmful bacteria and infections. Blood's clotting agents prevent loss of blood whenever blood vessels are injured by cuts or abrasions.

Lymphatic and endocrine systems

The lymphatic system assists the blood by its ability to travel into areas that blood cannot pass within the body. Lymph delivers nutrients and eliminating waste from the body's cells. Lymph acts a transport for nourishment from the blood to the body's cells. Lymph also is important in providing a defense against bacteria and toxins that invade the body. Lymph removes waste products from the blood cells and transports this waste back to the blood to be eliminated. Lymph is ideal for its purpose in providing an appropriate liquid surrounding for the body's cells.

The endocrine system works to secrete hormones into the blood stream produced by the pituitary gland, thyroid gland, and the ovaries. This glandular structure works directly with the body's nervous system to control and regulate numerous organs and systems within the body.

Lymph

The lymphatic system or lymph-vascular system is comprised of lymph spaces, lymph vessels, and lymph glands. This structure assists the blood system in a number of ways. Lymph is a yellowish, thin liquid created from the plasma found in the blood. This liquid is created through a process of filtration. The plasma is filtered through the capillary walls into the tissue spaces. In turn, the tissue found in the tissue spaces provides all the cells with a nutritive substance and takes out the compounds to be eliminated due to the metabolic processes. From this stage the liquid is absorbed into the lymphatic or lymph capillaries to be developed into lymph. The fluid produced from this is called lymph. Lymph goes through a detoxification by travel through the lymph nodes. Once it has been detoxified it can be safely reintroduced into the blood circulatory system.

Excretory system

The excretory system is the structure used throughout the body for purification and elimination of waste by-products. These by-products are eliminated through the kidneys, liver, skin, intestines, and lungs. The body goes through a process of purification as each organ performs its specific job in eliminating these waste by-products. The metabolism of cells produces harmful, poisonous compounds that must be discarded from the body to prevent illness. Urine is excreted by the kidneys as part of this purification and elimination process. Likewise, the liver releases bile. Persons who have a non-functioning liver may appear yellow or jaundice. Perspiration is the way that the skin assists in this process. The large intestine relinquishes decomposed and undigested food from the body. The lungs are used to exhale the compound carbon dioxide. Removal of these toxins is necessary to ensure good health.

Digestive system

The digestive system changes food eaten into a soluble form that can be used for energy within the cells of the body. Digestion is used to describe the process that is used to change the food that is eaten into a soluble form. A soluble form means that it is a form that can be used by the body. The mouth is first area that food passes and it is the beginning of the digestive process. Food travels from the mouth into the pharynx. Food travels from the pharynx to the esophagus or food pipe. The stomach has more enzymes that behave as catalyst to speed up a chemical transformation changing food into a more soluble form. Strong emotions, agitation, tension, and fatigue can be factors that disrupt digestion. Feelings of happiness and relaxation are factors in producing a healthy digestive process.

Respiratory system

The respiratory system includes the diaphragm and the lungs. This system is located in the upper portion of your body known as your chest cavity. The chest cavity is protected by a bony structure known as ribs. Breathing is regulated by the diaphragm. This muscular partition regulates the breathing rhythms. The diaphragm separates the chest from the abdominal region as added protection. Beneath the diaphragm are two organs known as lungs. Lungs are elastic tissues compiled of tiny cells that capture air. Inhalation allows oxygen to be absorbed into the blood stream. Exhalation allows carbon dioxide to be expelled. Suffocation is a term used to describe a person dying from a lack of oxygen. When you breathe through your nose air is warmed by the surface capillaries. Bacteria are filtered by the hairs found in the mucous membranes of the nasal passages.

Nail Anatomy and Physiology

Nail unit components

The first component of the nail unit is the matrix bed, constructing the nail plate. It appearance is in the shape of a white moon just beneath the nail plate. The visible part is called the lunula. The second component of the nail unit is the part that extends from the free edge to just beyond the fingertip. This is called the nail plate. The third component is the cuticular system. It is comprised of the eponychium and the hyponychium. The eponychium is the cuticle. True cuticle refers to living tissue, continuing under the proximal nail fold and back to its originating base point. This portion protects the area from injury and infection. It is under the nail plate where the free edge nail attaches to underlying tissues.

The fourth component describes the nail bed resting under the nail plate on the upper side of the distal phalanx or the end of the finger or toe. The bed epithelium is the thin layer of tissue which fastens the nail bed. The distal end of the nail bed joins with the bed epithelium to meet the hyponychium. This cornified material forms a grayish band which is known as onychodermal band or solehorn of the nail. The fifth component fastens the nail bed and the matrix bed to the underlying bone. Ligaments are found at the proximal feature of the matrix bed and the brink of the nail bed, joining to the region under the nail grooves. The sixth component of the nail unit is the nail folds; this refers to the skin that surrounds the nail plate.

Functions, growth rates, and growth conditions

The functions of the nail are multiple. However, the nail is useful for picking up and holding small objects. The nail may be used to scratch surfaces. The nail functions as a protective covering on the ends of your fingers and toes. The nail is useful for grooming purposes. The nail growth is affected by age, gender, disease, and temperature, although a healthy nail can grow at 0.1 mm per day or approximately 3mm per month. Toe nails will grow at about half that rate. Cold temperatures impact this growth negatively, while heat has a positive effect on the rate of growth. Men's nails usually grow at a more rapid pace than a female. Diseases may retard growth; however psoriasis has the opposite effect. Family members usually grow at approximately the same rate of speed.

Chemical content

The nail is comprised of magnesium, sodium, potassium, iron, copper, zinc, sulfur, and nitrogen. The organic compounds or amino acids which are present in the nail are sulfur and nitrogen. There is some trace of calcium in nails, but it is not useful in strengthening the nail. The other organic compounds found within the nail make up the stringy protein known as keratin. The keratin used to form the nail is harder than the keratin used to form the skin and hair. Nails are porous and will absorb water. The appearances of a dry, hard nail are deceptive as nail plates contain approximately 10-30 percent water. The water content is essential in allowing flexibility. Brittle nails have lower water content. One way to avoid or reduce water content is to apply an ointment based nail conditioner or nail enamel to the nail.

Nail disorders

Problem areas

Nail plate disorders can affect the matrix bed. Small white spots known as leuconychia may be visible under the shell of the nail plate. The whole nail may appear either excessively thick or abnormally thin. Ruts or crests running from one side to the other are rate-of-growth disturbances affecting all of the matrix bed are known as Beau's Lines. These usually occur after acute illness, high fevers, or brutal injuries. Possibly, only one nail is involved in an injury or trauma causing damage to the offending nail. Additionally, nail bed disorders are usually caused by a disconnected onycholysis or disconnection of the underlying tissue. Debris and callus build ups can exacerbate this problem. Distortional or misalignment irregularity of the bed plate may indicate bed epithelium wounds or ailments. Bed epithelial problems can contribute to onycholysis.

Eponychial disorders, hyponychial disorders, and injuries or chronic infections

Eponychial disorders and hyponychial disorders occur when there are surface disorders on the nail plate or under the free edge. However, whenever there is an abnormal adherence of the skin to the nail plate this indicates this type of disorder has occurred. If the shape of the underlying bone is impacted by a disease or an injury then this may indicate that the condition has detrimentally impacted the nail folds. The shape and the texture of the nail plate may have changed or deformed. Feet receive more stresses than hands. Additionally, warm, moist conditions may complicate the care and treatment of the feet. These conditions may be the underlying cause of the condition in the first place. Some conditions may be serviced. However, the golden rule must be applied before performing any nail care applications.

Hangnails and melanonychia

Another name for hangnails is agnails; a condition that results from dry cuticles or cuticles that were trimmed too aggressively. The treatment for this disorder involves applying oil to soften the cuticles, followed by the use of nippers to trim off the hangnail. Hangnails are prone to infection, if proper treatment is not applied.

The nail disorder melanonychia appears black under the nail plate or as part of the nail plate. This may affect a portion or the entire nail. Melanocytes or pigment cells in the proximal matrix bed distribute the melanin that appears black. The blackened color increases as the nail grows towards the free edge. This is common in races with dark skin. If a fair skin individual has this condition, they should be seen by a physician to rule out malignant melanoma. Nail treatment can be given.

Furrows

Furrows are also known as corrugations which appear as long ridges the run across the nail. The ridges can run in either direction. This condition is a part of the aging process, but may be indicative of psoriasis, poor circulation, or frostbite. Other physical conditions that lead to this nail disorder are high fevers, pregnancy, injury, measles, or zinc deficiency. The nail can be treated if there is no broken skin or deep ruts. Do not use a metal pusher around the cuticle. A cotton tip orange wood stick should be gently applied around the cuticle. Use a fine grit buffer to gently buff the nails to take away the corrugated look across the nails. If additional ridges remain, then use ridge filler and an application of colored nail polish. This treatment will improve the nails' appearance.

Onychauxis and trumpet nails

Onychauxis or hypertrophy appears as a nail disorder where the nails grow overly thick, not thin like persons with the disorder onychatrophia. Internal imbalance, infections, injury, or heredity may have contributed to this nail disorder. File the nail until it is smooth; follow with buffing and pumice powder.

Trumpet nails or pincer nail disorders result from nail growth abnormalities. The nail grows towards the edge and curls inward. The nail can grow into itself, forming the shape of a cone or a trumpet, hence its name. This condition can be painful to the underlying nail bed and the distal skin. This condition usually affects the toes, but can, affect the fingers. Tight fitting shoes or a bone spur can be the cause. The nail should be trimmed to alleviate any discomfort. A referral to a physician may be necessary.

Leuconychia and onychatrophia

Leuconychia is a nail disorder that results from air bubbles, bruises, or injuries of the nail. This nail disorder develops as tiny white spots on the nail. There is no known treatment for this condition; however the nail can be trimmed as it grows to remove the spots. Nail care treatments can be applied to hide the condition.

The nail disorder onychatrophia is also known as atrophy. The nail is wasting away from injury or internal disease. The appearance of the nail is lusterless, shrunken, and may fall off. Extreme caution is warranted. The nail must be filed with the fine side of the emery board. Metal pushers, strong soaps, or washing powders should be avoided. If the nail falls off from a disease that has been cured successfully, then it is possible that the nail could grow back again.

Onychocryptosis

Onychocryptosis is the name given for ingrown nails that grow into the sides of the tissue around the nail. The nail disorder is caused from the matrix bed folding into the soft tissues around the nail. Precursors to this disorder may be plicatured nails and tile-shaped nails. The foot is particularly susceptible to this problem due to the stresses that are placed upon the foot. The penetration of the soft tissue allows an entry point for bacteria to form. This causes an acute infection known as paronychia. Paronychia or acute infection normally results from Staphylococcus. Redness, extreme pain, and a small abscess or pus pocket can form on the distal end of the digit infected. Treatment from a podiatrist is required. The nail technician should only trim the nail if the tissue in not infected surrounding the nail.

Tile shaped nails and plicatured nails

Tile shaped nail describes the nail disorder that curves into the matrix bed. This curvature is evident along the nail plate. The client should not have pain associated with this condition. The nail care treatment can be applied without concern.

The nail disorder known as plicatured nail involves an abnormal growth. This can be attributed to an injury or heredity. The abnormality originates in the matrix bed. The nail plate will develop in a plicatured manner. Additionally, this condition may lead to the growth of an ingrown toenail. Tight shoes may cause the nail to remold and fold the matrix bed into this abnormal shape. Nail treatment can be safely applied. The technician should carefully round out the corners of the plicatured nail. Ingrown toe nails may require the treatment of a physician.

Onychogryphosis

Onychogryphosis is the technical term given for ram's horn nail. Matrix bed injury or heredity can be a leading cause for this nail disorder. The big toe is most susceptible, although all toes and fingernails may be affected by this disorder. The nail is of a brownish coloration. The odd growth of this nail results in a thick, curvature that resembles the horn of a ram. This thick growth is difficult to trim. The nail should be trimmed regularly as this is not a condition that has a cure. There should be no infection at time of nail treatment. Once this is established, then the technician should use nail nippers and a file to trim the nail. The grooves in the nail are symptoms of areas of weakness. The nail should be trimmed in small chunks to prevent breakage.

Onychophagy, onychophosis, onychophyma, and onychorrhexis

Onychophagy is the term for nails that have grown abnormally because of excessive biting. Routine manicures with the application of artificial tips and wraps may be applied. Onychophosis is the technical name given to describe the growth of horny epithelium in the nail bed. Onychophyma is the technical name given to describe the condition onychauxis. Onychauxis is has the symptoms of puffiness and swelling associated with the nail. Onychorrhexis is the technical name given to describe split or brittle nails. These nails typically have a series of lengthwise ridges. This condition can result from injury, abrasive cuticle solvents, nail polish removers, and aggressive filing techniques. The treatment recommended involves the softening of the nails with a reconditioning treatment. Future applications of abrasive soaps, nail polish removers, and aggressive filing techniques are to be avoided.

Onychosis and dorsal pterygium

Onychosis is a disorder known as onychopathy which refers to the terminology nail disease.

Pterygium of the nail has the appearance of disfigurement of the proximal nail fold (eponychium) or the distal nail fold (hyponychium). Dorsal pterygium is the term used to describe the condition that affects the top of the nail plate. The deformity appears as the skin of the eponychium and the true cuticle fastens to the nail plate. A winged appearance is the result. The cuticle sometimes attaches itself to the matrix bed. The nail plate may fall off. Dorsal pterygium may be caused by lichen planus or rheumatoid arthritis. Lichen planus is a skin disease. The nail care technician may gently massage the affected area with cuticle creams and conditions. Unfortunately, little can be done to reverse the affects of this nail disorder.

Mold

Mold or fungus is a nail disorder resulting from an infection that starts as a yellowish-green coloration. The nail may blacken. Some clinicians attribute the greenish coloration to a growth of bacteria known as Pseudomonas aeruginosa. Pseudomonas aeruginosa is found in soil and water. Open wounds are particular susceptible to this bacterium. Mold or bacteria may work itself between the artificial nail and nail plate. The nail technician will have to remove the artificial nail to expose the nail plate. The nail plate will need to be sanitized with a disinfectant. The artificial nail should not be reapplied until all evidence of the mold or bacteria is gone. The treatment by a physician may be necessary should the condition persist. The technician should follow all proper sanitizing and disinfecting procedures to prevent the infection from spreading as it is contagious.

Onychomycosis tinea unguium and onycholysis

Onychomycosis tinea unguium is the result of a disease brought on by contact with fungi. Fungi are vegetable parasites that are opportunistic, which means that they take advantage of the weak. Disease or injury may cause the nail to be more susceptible to these opportunistic fungal infections. Dark, moist, warm places are ideal for growth. A whitish growth is known as Leukonychia Mycotica. Other fungi growths may be yellow, black, or brown.

Onycholysis permits the nail to disengage itself from the nail bed. Disengagement usually begins at the free edge and works itself up towards the lunula. The nail does not normally fall off. Internal disorders, trauma, infection, and medications can contribute to this condition. Coloration and nail bed thickness may result. The nail technician should refer the client for treatment by a licensed physician.

Ventral pterygium

The reversal of the condition dorsal pterygium is known as ventral pterygium. Ventral pterygium means that the hyponychium has attached itself to underside of the nail plate. The distal nail groove is destroyed allowing the hyponychium to grow bulkier. The nail should be examined along the free edge to prevent the ventral pterygium from being trimmed along with the nail. The nail should only be trimmed when the nail technician has a clear view of the nail and the ventral pterygium. The nails on the foot are particular susceptible to this disorder. Hereditary factors, Raynaud's disease, arteriosclerosis and other bone diseases may contribute to the condition of ventral pterygium. The nail care technician may gently massage the affected area with cuticle creams and conditions. Unfortunately, little can be done to reverse the affects of this nail disorder.

Onychoptosis and paronychia

Onychoptosis describes the nail disorder that causes the nail to shed occasionally. Syphilis, fever, system disorders, trauma, and medication can lead to this disorder.

Paronychia is caused by an infection. Fungi or yeast may infect the tissues around or underneath the nail plate. Redness, swelling, soreness, and small pockets of pus are symptoms of the infection. This condition may begin at the base of the nail, around the nail, or at the tip of the nail. A name that describes the infection of the entire nail is runaround. Yeast infection or candida may lead to chronic paronychia. Nails and cuticles should be gently treated; removing only dead cuticle is advised. Proper sanitation and disinfection procedures should be explicitly followed to prevent contagions from spreading.

Onychomadesis and pyogenic granuloma

Pyogenic granuloma appears a red growth. This is an inflammation and should not be treated.

Onychomadesis causes the nail plate to shed. The nail plate may be affected on the toes or on the fingernails. Infection, a minor injury, aggressive filing, or a systemic injury can cause this disorder. Chemotherapy or x-rays used in the treatment of cancer patients have been known to lead to this disorder. Systemic disease may impact all of the nails on the client. However, localized injuries may only impact one nail. Shedding occurs when production of the nail plate is prevented. Beau's lines are evident. A groove forms that allows the plate to separate from the matrix bed. Sometimes, the disease that caused this condition is cured or the injury is healed. A new nail plate may grow. Cautious, gentle treatment should be applied when filing. Polish should not be applied as this may seal in any infectious elements.

Nail disorder symptoms

Nail disorders are characterized by injury to the nail, sickness, or imbalances within the body. The professional nail technician should be able to recognize the symptoms associated with a nail disorder. This knowledge will empower the nail technician to make the appropriate decision in whether or not performance of a nail treatment is warranted. The diagnosis of a nail disorder should always be performed by a licensed physician, but you can tell a client that they may have a problem and should seek medical assistance. In less serious cases, a cosmetic treatment will improve the appearance of the nails. The golden rule of nail care is to refer the customer to the physician if the skin in infected, inflamed, broken or swollen. Red and soreness in the area indicates an inflammation. Pus is present in most infections. Broken skin is cut or torn.

Fingernail infections

A type of infection that appears white or discolored can occur under the nail plate. This infection can spread towards the cuticle. The discoloration may remain white or it may darken as the infection develops. A client may have the fungus present on his or her hands, feet, or nails. This contagious condition requires treatment by a physician. Clients should be referred to their doctor to obtain medical treatment promptly. A nail care treatment should not be applied. However, a client may request that an artificial nail is removed. This will eliminate any barrier to the natural nail. Remember to wear gloves. All orangewood sticks, abrasives, and porous products should be discarded immediately to prevent any contagious bacteria from spreading in your work area. Follow disinfectant procedures thoroughly before servicing another client.

Bruised nails, discolored nails, and eggshell nails

A smashed nail may form a blood clot in the matrix bed or nail bed. The color will appear black or maroon, often the nail will fall off on its own. The application of artificial nails is not acceptable. Discolored nails may appear yellow, blue, blue-grey, red, and purple in color. This discoloration may be one symptom of systemic disorders, poor blood circulation, a heart condition, or the use of certain topical or oral medications. It is acceptable to hide this condition with artificial tips, wraps or a colored nail polish. Eggshell nails are thin and white, bent along the free edge of the nail. Improper diet, internal disease, medication, or nervous disorders may contribute to this condition. Extreme caution should be used to prevent breakage; gently filing with the fine side of an emery board.

Basic Chemistry and Product Function

Light and evaporation

The method that the initiator molecule gains energy is through light or heat. Ultraviolet light is a form of energy used by light-cured enhancement products. It is essential to store these products away from the source of energy to prevent the process of polymerization. Nail polishes, topcoats and base coats do not go through the polymerization process. Instead, they work through a physical reaction caused by evaporation. The volatile polymers used are not cross linked and tend to dissolve quite rapidly. The solvents evaporate leaving behind a smooth polymer covering or sheet. The strength of this covering is reduced due to the lack of cross linked enhancements present. The key to a healthy nail is good care of the nail plate and proper techniques applied by a skilled, educated nail care professional.

Adhesives and primers

Adhesives are applied by the nail technician in different forms. Epoxy resins and high tech cyanoacrylate are used by nail technicians. Erroneously these adhesives are sometimes, referred to as glue, which can be a misleading terminology. A primer is applied to assist the adhesive process. If a client has problem oily skin a nail technician may apply a nail primer to cause the nail enhancement to fasten more securely to the nail plate. Nail technicians should use caution to prevent the skin from coming into contact with primers or other corrosive substances. The corrosive chemical in primers is methacrylic acid. Only a thin coat of primer is recommended to prevent harmful effects to the nail plate. The nail plate is harmed through saturation. Saturation can cause burning of the skin. Some non-corrosive primers do not contain methacrylic acid.

Catalysts and solvents

The alteration of a molecule is caused by the assistance of an energy source. Heat and/or light cause a chemical reaction. A nail technician will use a chemical or a catalyst to cause this chemical reaction to occur more rapidly. Examples of the catalysts used by nail technicians are in U. V. gels and in monomer liquids. The catalyst used for wraps is applied with a spray, dopper, or brush. Solvents are substances used to dissolve or soften another substance. Water is referred to as the universal solvent due to its frequent, wide range of use. Acetone is another solvent used quite often by a nail technician. In cases where acetones or other solvents have been used extensively, it is recommended to reduce the solvent strength to lessen the effect of natural oil removal from the nail.

Fingernail coatings and polymerizations

Fingernail coatings include nail polishes, top coats, artificial enhancements and adhesives. One type of coating consists of a chemical reaction that cures or polymerize like those found in artificial enhancements. Another type is hardened by vaporization from a physical reaction such as nail polish and top coats. The words cure, curing, or hardening is used to describe the chemical reactions that occur when polymers form massive chains of molecules. These chains usually form a solid surface as those found in Teflon, nylon, hair, nail plates, or wood. Products found in the salon have monomers that are waiting for initiator molecules to begin the process of polymerizations. Wraps and tip adhesives form simple polymer chains. Applications that produce a simple polymer chain may be damaged more easily by stains, impact, or heavy stresses. A cross-linker product has the ability to strengthen the nail enhancement process.

Products applied to the nail

Nail bleach can be utilized in the removal of yellow stains from the nail plate and from under the free edge of the nail. Nail whiteners with zinc oxide or titanium dioxide are also useful in changing the nail to a whitish color. These products come in a paste, a cream, a coated string, and in pencil forms. Nail polish can be obtained in a dry form or a liquid form. Colored polishes add sheen to the nail when applied in two coats. The nitrocellulose or volatile solvent in the colored polish can dry quickly. However, some have the additive castor oil to slow this process. The base coat has no color and can be applied to the natural nail. The base coat is made from either of these chemicals: ethyl acetate, a solvent, isopropyl alcohol, butyl acetate, nitrocellulose, and sometimes formaldehyde.

Powdered alum or styptic powder is useful to prevent the minor flow of blood. Do not handle the blood or to allow the blood to contaminate other surfaces. Apply the powder on the end of cotton tipped orangewood stick. Soap is a common product which is useful for cleaning your hands and that of your client's. Soap can be flaked, beaded, caked, or liquid. However, liquid is recommended due to its more hygienic form. A cake of soap is surface which conceals and allows bacteria to grow. Organic solvents and acetone, with the occasional mixture of oil is used as a nail polish remover solvent. However, non-acetone remover is recommended for clients with artificial nails. Cuticle creams and oils lubricate dry cuticles and brittle nails. Cuticle solvents, (a 2-5% sodium or potassium hydroxide plus glycerin), are used in cuticle removals.

Important terms

Adhesion: molecules on one surface are attracted to the molecules on another surface with the end result of both surfaces fastening to each other.

Adhesive: gummy chemical that results in the union of two surfaces that do not have a molecular attraction to each other.

Catalyst: a chemical that causes a chemical reaction to occur more rapidly.

Chemical: everything that is not made of energy is made up of some type of chemical composition.

Chemical change: the alteration of one chemical into another kind of chemical or substance.

Chemical reaction: when a molecule alters its structure with the assistance of an energy source. One example of a chemical change occurs when artificial nail enhancements must have light or heat to produce the desired transformation.

Corrosive: a substance that has harmful effects on the skin and/or nail bed tissue.

Antiseptics: effective sanitizing solutions and can be used on the skin.

Contaminated: surfaces and/or objects that are polluted by foreign substances like dust, cleansers, dirt or bacteria.

Contaminant: foreign substances that exist on the surface of an object.

Decontamination: destroy, reduce, or control the contaminants and pathogens on surfaces.

Disinfection: decontamination that can eliminate pathogens on surfaces and objects.
Disinfectants: strong, professional-strength solutions used to decontaminate and to control the existence of pathogens on surfaces and objects.

Pathogens: approximately 30 percent of all germs which can cause disease or infections.

Sterilization: put an end to or eliminate all the contaminants that live on a surface or on an object.

Sanitation: cleaning method used to lower the existence of pathogens or contaminants in the salon.

Sanitizers: A solution used to lower the existence of contaminants on a surface or object. Soap and water can be an effective sanitizer.

Acquired Immune Deficiency Syndrome (AIDS): this is caused by the HIV virus. This virus is reportedly not transferred by casual contact, but rather by the transfer of bodily fluids. HIV can be transmitted through sexual contact with an infected person or through the shared used of dirty hypodermic needles. A mother can transfer this disease during pregnancy to her unborn child. Some blood transfusions have resulted in transmission of this disease, although safety precautions are more widely known and followed now.

Asepsis: freedom of toxins or poisons in the blood or other tissues of pathogenic or germ infected microorganisms.

Bacilli: this variety has a rod-shape. Some diseases common to this bacterium include tetanus, typhoid, tuberculosis, and diphtheria.

Bacteria: one-celled microorganisms found in water, air, dust, lint, and decaying substances. Most bacteria are harmless, but some can cause serious illnesses.

Infection: this occurs when body tissue is attacked by disease causing microorganisms such as bacteria, viruses, and fungi.

Microorganisms: single-cell, life forms that are too small to be seen with the naked eye.

Mitosis: reproduction of bacteria cells. Reproduction occurs when a mature cell splits into two cells.

Natural barrier: the skin and its mantle are two protections that we have against infection.

Nonpathogenic: this bacterium is classified as not harmful and helps to produce food and oxygen. The digestive tract contains a nonpathogenic bacterium that helps break down the food and enzymes.

Parasites: animal parasites which live off living substances. Ringworm, scabies, itch-mite, and pediculosis (lice) are examples of parasitic organisms.

Pathogenic: about 30% of all types of bacteria classified as disease causing, producing poisons or toxins in tissue. Another term used to refer to pathogens is germs.

Cocci: one of the three main types of pathogenic bacteria that appears as a round, pus-producing bacteria. Staphylococci, streptococci, and diplococcic are all types of cocci or pus-producing bacteria.

Cilia: hair like projections that bacteria use to travel through liquid.

Contagious: a state of being that can easily transmit a disease or infection to another person.

Diplococcic: a pus-producing bacteria variety that grows in pairs and can cause pneumonia.

Flagella: hair like projections that bacteria use to travel through liquid.

Fungi: this parasite presents a risk to nail care as fungi can be transferred from nail to nail.

Germs: another term used to describe pathogens.

Immunity: the defense system designed to resist diseases or infection.

Immunocompromised: a weaken state in the immune system that causes a person to be more susceptible to a disease or an infection.

Rickettsia: these small organisms are carried by fleas, ticks, and lice that can cause typhus or Rocky Mountain spotted fever.

Sepsis: the existence of toxins or poisons in the blood or other tissues of pathogenic microorganisms.

Spirilla: these bacteria are spiral or corkscrew-shaped. Syphilis is caused by the spirilla bacteria treponema pallida.

Staphylococci: a pus-producing bacteria variety that grows in clusters. This variety exists in local infections, such as sores, abscesses, and boils.

Streptococci: a pus-producing bacteria variety that grows in chains. This variety may spread strep throat, rheumatic fever, blood poisoning, and other infections, or diseases.

Toxins: poisons produced by pathogens or germs.

Viruses: Hepatitis, chicken pox, influenza, measles, mumps, and the common cold are caused by these pathogenic agents. These contagious agents are smaller than bacteria and are transferred by contact with a person with the infectious disease.

Anatomy: the stud of the structure of the body and its parts.

Cells: the basic building blocks of life forms. All living things are made from cells.

Protoplasm: a colorless, gelatinous matter that contains food fundamentals such as protein, fat, carbohydrates, and mineral salts. The protoplasm is made up of the nucleus, cytoplasm, centrosome, and cell membrane.

Nucleus: the center of the cell which is vital to cell reproduction.

Cytoplasm: the outside of the nucleus that is responsible for food elements needed for growth, reproduction, and self-repair of the cell.

Centrosome: the small, part of the cytoplasm that has an impact of the reproduction of the cell.

Cell membrane: this controls the transportation of matter in and out of the cell.

Metabolism: a complex chemical method that allows the body cells to be fed and provided with energy.

Brain: this controls the organs in the body and its systems.

Heart: controls the transportation of the blood's circulatory system.

Lungs: used to supply oxygen to the blood throughout the body.

Liver: used to remove toxins from the digestive system in the body.

Kidneys: used to excrete water and other waste products out of the body.

Stomach and Intestines: used to digest food and excrete waste products out of the body.

System: There are ten structures or systems in the body. Each forms a group of organs with its own specific function.

Nervous system: group of organs controls and coordinates the workings of all the others systems within the body.

Circulatory system: purpose of this structure is to provide and transport blood throughout the body.

Endocrine system: the purpose of this structure is comprised of the ductless glands that secrete hormones into the bloodstream.

Excretory system: purpose of this group of organs is to remove waste from the body.

Respiratory system: group of organs responsible to carry and supply oxygen within the body.

Digestive system: group of organs that changes food materials into energy used by the cells within the body.

Reproductive system: group of organs is responsible for allowing human beings to reproduce offspring.

Integumentary System: two layered, protective covering that is responsible for the sensory reception of the body and for regulating the body's temperature.

Skeletal system: the bony framework of the body that is useful for the purpose of protection, support and movement.

Muscular system: flesh that covers the skeletal system and produces movement.

Tissues: a grouping of cells of the same type. Each tissue has a specific function and is characterized by its form.

Connective tissue: this grouping of cells functions to support, protect, and bind together tissues of the body. Bones, cartilage, ligament, tendon, fascia, and fat tissue are the connective tissue of the body.

Muscular tissue: this grouping of cells forms the muscles of the body.

Nerve tissue: this grouping of cells in responsible to carry messages to and from the brain to control and coordinate the body functions.

Epithelial tissue-the grouping of cells forms the protective covering of the body like skin, mucous membranes, and linings of the ear, digestive and respiratory organs, and glands.

Liquid tissue: this grouping of cells carries the food, waste products, and hormones through the bloods circulatory system and the lymph system.

Os: medical term for bones.

Osteocytes: hard connective tissue which consists of bone cells.

Periosteum: Specialized connective tissue covering the bones and assisting in bone restoration after injury.

Cartilage: a tough elastic material which cushions bones and resembles bone without the mineral content.

Ligaments: strengthen the joint. These are useful in movement.

Joints: part of the body where the bone meets at a junction.

Joint capsule: provides a sack like structure at the connective junction.

Synovial fluid: liquid in the joint that lubricates and nourishes the joint and surrounding cartilage.

Pivot joints: an example of this is found in the neck where one bone turns on another bone.

Hinge joints: an example of this is found in the elbow or knee where two bones connect similar to a hinge on a door frame.

Metacarpals: name of the five bones in the hand and palm.

Phalanges: thumb has these two bones and the fingers have three bones, making a total of fourteen bones in all.

Femur: heavy, length of bone which is found above the knee.

Tibia: bone found on the inside of the leg that begins at the ankle and ends just below the knee.

Fibula: bone found on the outside of the leg, beginning at the ankle and ending just below the knee.

Patella: accessory bone that forms the knee cap joint.

Talus: one of the three bones that make up the ankle joint. The other two bones of the ankle joint are the tibia, and fibula.

Tarsal: there are seven types, (talus, calcaneus, navicular, and three cuneiform bones, and the cuboid), which make up the foot, totaling 26 in all.

Ball-and-socket joint: an example of this is found in the hip where one bone is rounded and fits into the hollow of another bone.

Gliding joints: an example of this is found in the ankle where two bones glide over each other in movement.

Scapula: this is the name of one of the bones found in the shoulder.

Clavicle: this is the name of the bone found in the shoulder, also known as the collar bone.

Humerus: this is the largest, top portion of the arm.

Ulna: this is the large bone found on the underside of the forearm.

Radius: this is the small bone found on the inside of the forearm.

Carpus: this is comprised of a flexible joint with eight small, irregular bones that are held in a group by ligaments called the wrist.

Deltoid: large, bulky triangular muscle encasing the shoulder allowing movement, turning the arm.

Biceps: two points of attachment located on the forearm responsible for the movement of flexing the elbow and turning the palms upward.

Triceps: three points of attachment muscle that covers the back of the arm which permits the movement of the upper arm and allows extension of the arm.

Forearm: the part of the arm containing a series of muscles and tendons.

Pronator: the part of the muscle which turns the hand inward and the palm down.

Supinator: the part of the muscle which turns the hand outward and the palm upright.

Flexors: the part of the muscle which bends the wrist, turning the hand upright, and closes the fingers.

Extensor: the part of the muscle which straightens out the wrist, the hand and the fingers.

Metatarsal: the 14 bones called phalanges which form the toes. The big toe has two phalanges, and the other toes each have three phalanges.

Myology: the study of the structure and functions of the muscles, including the study of the muscular diseases.

Striated muscles: muscles found in the face, arm, and leg that can move voluntarily.

Non-striated muscles: muscles found in the stomach and intestines that move involuntarily.

Cardiac muscle: the muscle which describes the heart.

Belly: a collection of muscle fibers which form a typical striated muscle.

Tendon: used to attach the end of the bone or other structure to the belly.

Origin: the description of the part of the muscle that has a fixed or less mobile attachment.

Insertion: the description of the part of the muscle that has a more mobile attachment.

Abductors: the muscles located at the base of the thumbs and fingers which separate the fingers.

Extensor digitorum longus: the muscle that moves the foot upward and allows extension of the toes.

Tibialis anterior: the muscles located on the front part of the shin that is responsible for moving the foot upward and inward.

Peroneus longus: the muscles covering the external side of the calf that inverts the foot and allows movement in the downward position.

Peroneus brevis: the muscles located on the lower surface of the fibula that allows the foot to move down and outward.

Gastrocnemius: the muscles located on the lower rear surface of the heel that pulls the foot in a downward motion.

Soleus: muscles located at the upper portion of the fibula that move the foot in a downward motion.

Nerve impulses: muscle tissue is stimulated to produce these pulsations throughout the nervous system.

Massage: muscle tissue is stimulated through hand massage techniques or through an electric vibrator.

Electric current: muscle tissue stimulated through the application of measured electrical shocks applied to the muscle area to produce visible muscle contractions.

Light rays: muscle tissue can be stimulated through the use of infrared and ultraviolet rays.

Heat rays: muscle tissue can be stimulated through the use of heating lamps and heating caps.

Moist heat: muscle tissue can be stimulated through the use of steamers or moderately warm steam towels placed directly on the muscles.

Chemicals: certain acids and salts used to stimulate the muscles.

Pressure: term used to describe the motion of the massage from the insertion point to the origin point of the muscle.

Peripheral system: sensory and motor nerve fibers responsible for transporting messages to and from the central nervous system.

Autonomic nervous system: system responsible for the unconscious regulation of the smooth muscles, glands, blood vessels, and the heart.

Sympathetic system: useful during stressful, vigorous, or emergency situations and is part of the autonomic nervous system.

Parasympathetic systems: useful during routine, restful, energy-conserving situations and is part of the autonomic nervous system.

Brain: the principal accumulation of nerve tissue in the body which performs as the central processing component stored in the cranium.

Spinal cord: this formation of nerve cells comes out from the brain and extends to the trunk of the body. This cord is encased in a bony structure known as the spinal column.

Neuron: the main structural nerve cell of the nervous system.

Extensor digitorum brevis: the muscles in the foot.

Abductor hallucis: the muscles in the foot.

Flexor digitorum brevis: the muscles in the foot.

Adductors: muscles located at the base of the thumbs and fingers which draw the fingers together.

Neurology: the study of the nervous system and its disorders.

Nerves: fine fibers that make up the nervous systems in helping to control and coordinate its functions.

Nervous system: this part of the body controls and manages the functions of all the systems and synchronizes their work. A technician should recognize how the effects of massage stimulate the nerves in the feet, legs, hands, arms, and the entire body.

Cerebro-spinal: the brain and spinal cord works to control the mental functioning, the five senses, (smelling, seeing, tasting, feeling, and hearing), and the voluntary muscle actions of the body and face.

Ulnar nerve: mass of long, white bands of neurons and its branches which transport messages to the outer part of the arm and palm of the hand.

Radial nerve: mass of long, white bands of neurons and its branches which transport messages to the inside part of the arm and the back of the hand.

Median nerve: smaller mass of long, white bands of neurons and its branches which transport messages to the arm and the hand.

Digital nerve: mass of long, white bands of neurons and its branches which transport messages to the fingers in the hand.

Tibial nerve: part of the sciatic nerve that follows along behind the knee and responsible for transporting messages to the knee, the muscles of the calf, the skin of the leg, the sole, heel, and underside of the toes.

Nerves: a mass of long, white bands of neurons which transport messages to and from the brain to diverse parts of the body.

Sensory nerves: known also as afferent nerves which transport impulses from the sense organs to the brain. These afferent nerves produce sensations of touch, cold, heat, sight, hearing, taste, smell, pain, and pressure.

Motor nerves: known also as efferent nerves that function to transport impulses from the brain to the muscles in the production of movements.

Mixed nerves: the combination of sensory and motor fibers that serves a dual purpose in sending and receiving messages.

Receptors: the sensory nerve endings near the skin's surface that serve to transfer impulses from the sensory nerves to the brain and back over the motor nerves to the muscles.

Reflex: automatic, spontaneous movement resulting from a stimulus transmitting an impulse.

Dorsal cutaneous nerve: also known as the dorsal found on the top of the foot.

Saphenous nerve: band of neurons carrying impulses to the inside skin of the leg and foot.

Sural nerve: this band of neurons carries impulses to the outside skin on the backside of the foot and leg.

Dorsal nerve: band of neurons supplying impulses to the skin on the top of the foot.

Circulatory system: also known as the vascular system which controls the rhythm of the circulation of blood throughout the body by way of the arteries, veins and capillaries.

Blood-vascular system: structure forming the heart and blood vessels working to circulate the blood.

Lymph-vascular system: glands and vessels which circulates the lymph fluid into the bloodstream. This system is also known as the lymphatic system.

Lymph: yellow fluid in the lymphatic system.

Common peroneal nerve: this part of the sciatic nerve is a band of neurons which extends from the knee to make its way to the head of the fibula to the front of the leg where it divides into two pathways.

Deep peroneal nerve: also known as the anterior tibial nerve.

Anterior tibial nerve: this band of neurons extends down the front of the leg, behind the muscles carrying impulses to the muscles and skin on the top portion of the foot and beside the first and second toes.

Superficial peroneal nerve: also known as the musculo-cutaneous nerve.

Musculo-cutaneous nerve: band of neurons extends down the leg, under the skin carrying impulses to the muscles, the skin of the leg, toes, the skin of the toes, and the top portion of the foot.

Atria: name referring to the right and left atrium.

Auricle: also known as atrium.

Arteries: muscular, resilient thick hoses that transport oxygen filled blood from the heart to the capillaries of the body.

Capillaries: nourishment and waste products travel through these tiny, thin walled blood vessels that are connected to smaller arteries and veins.

Veins: these hoses are used to transport blood that has been depleted of oxygen back to the capillaries and the heart.

Blood vessels: are formed from the arteries, capillaries, and veins. These hoses are useful for carrying blood to and from the heart and to the tissues found within the body.

Blood: red, salty liquid that moves through the circulatory system furnishing nutrients.

Pulmonary circulation: this describes the blood that is circulated from the heart to the lungs for the purpose of purification.

Heart: muscular, funnel shaped pump found within the chest cavity.

Pericardium: this sheath or membrane enfolds around the heart.

Vagus: this consists of the tenth cranial nerve and nerves from the autonomic system which are responsible for the control and rhythm of heartbeats.

Right atrium: right uppermost compartment of the four chambers that forms the thin lining in the interior of the heart.

Left atrium: left uppermost compartment of the four chambers that forms the thin lining in the interior of the heart.

Right ventricle: right lower compartment of the four chambers that forms a thick lining in the interior of the heart.

Left ventricle: left lower compartment of the four chambers that forms a thick lining in the interior of the heart.

Valves: flaps that open and close, allowing blood flow in one direction.

Systemic circulation: this describes the blood that is circulated back and forth from the heart to various pathways throughout the entire body's circulatory structure.

General circulation: also known as systemic circulation.

Red corpuscles: red blood cells useful for transporting oxygen to the cells throughout the body.

Erythrocytes: also known as red blood cells or red corpuscles.

White corpuscles: the white blood cells or leucocytes that work to destroy the germs that may cause disease within the body.

Blood platelets: also known as thrombocytes. These are tinier than red blood cells and work as blood clotting agents within the blood.

Plasma: the yellowish fluid that assists in the flow of red and white blood cells and blood platelets. This fluid is responsible for transporting food and secretions to cells and transports carbon dioxide from the cells.

Ulnar arteries: pathways providing the outside of the arm and the palm of the hand with its main blood supply.

Radial arteries: pathways providing the inside of the arm and the back of the hand with its main blood supply.

Popliteal artery: artery having two separate pathways called anterior tibial and posterior tibial.

Anterior tibial: one of the pathways that provides the foot with its main blood supply. This pathway turns into the dorsalis pedis.

Posterior tibial: another pathway that provides the foot with its main blood supply.

Endocrine system: structure made from glands which secrete compounds into the blood supply.

Gland: specially designed organ that secretes compounds into the blood supply.

Hormones: chemicals that are secreted from the endocrine glands into the bloodstream. These chemicals impact the body's metabolism and its systems.

Eponychium: cuticle found on the underside shell of the proximal nail. It fastens to the top of the nail pate, extending out onto the nail as a slight, transparent band of stratum corneum or skin.

Hyponychium: the part that attaches to the underlying tissues of the nail and is found at the free edge of the nail or the distal. This part protects the area from external moisture, bacteria, or fungi.

Nail bed: part underneath the nail plate, positioned on top of the distal phalanx or the end of the finger or toe. The nail bed continues out from the lunula to the area just prior to the free edge of the nail.

Specialized ligaments: these fasten the nail bed and matrix bed to the underlying bone.

Nail folds: crease of normal skin that closes around the nail plate.

Onyx: hardest part of the skin or Integumentary system known as the nail.

Keratin: all parts of the skin are formed from this protein. Skin, hair, and nails are made from either soft or hard keratins.

Nail unit: comprised of six components including the matrix bed, nail plate, cuticular system, nail bed, specialized ligaments and the nail folds.

Matrix bed: cells that make up the nail plate running from under the proximal nail groove to the whitish part located underneath the nail plate. The part of the matrix bed that is most exposed is referred to as the lunula.

Nail plate: most exposed area formulated from the matrix cells. The free edge is the area described as the end of the nail plate that extends beyond the fingertips.

Cuticular system: comprised of the eponychium and the hyponychium.

Dermatology: study of the good physical shape of the skin and disorders that affect the condition of this health.

Elasticity: state of the skin that describes its ability to restore its original shape after being pulled away from the bone.

Epidermis: another name for epidermis is cuticle. This describes the exterior protective covering of the skin or the part that is visible to the eye.

Stratum corneum: also refer to as "horney layer"; this consists of a layer of dead, keratinized cells.

Stratum lucidum: a clear cell layer that is on the palms of the hands and soles of the feet.

Basal layer: another name for this is the stratum germination. This is formed of layers of cells that are shaped in various shapes. The deepest layer continues to produce new cells to replace the used up cells.

Adipose: fatty tissue that has a soft, smooth texture.

Subcutaneous tissue: tissue in the body that contains adipose. This tissue provides the body with a protective cushion for the exterior skin. Age, sex, and health are factors in the thickness of the skin.

Tactile corpuscles: nerve endings.

Motor nerves: cord like fibers or nerves responsible for the constriction or the expansion of blood vessels. This works in accord with the arrector pili muscles to produce a contraction movement.

Arrector pili muscles: this fastens itself to the hair follicles in order to produce a contraction movement. Goose bumps are a good example.

Secretory nerves: cord like fibers or nerves in the sweat and oil glands. Nerves in the sweat glands send impulses that cause the organ to secrete sweat. Nerves in the oil gland produce sebum.

Melanin: dark skin pigment that protects cells from the effects of harmful rays of the sun or ultraviolet.

Dermis: deep level of the skin comprised of blood vessels, lymph vessels, nerves, sweat glands, and oil glands referred to as the "true skin". The three parts of the dermis are derma, corium, and cortis.

Papillary layer: level of skin is found beneath the epidermis. Component of this layer is papillae, small blood vessels, nerve endings, and melanin.

Papillae: projections which stretch out rising into the epidermis.

Reticular layer: this level comprises fat cells, blood vessels, lymph vessels, sweat glands, oil glands, hair follicles, and the arrector pili muscles. The arrector pili muscles fasten to hair follicles.

Hypodermis: refers to fatty layer of skin called subcutis.

Nerve: rope fibers that transports messages from the organs to the central nervous system.

Sensory nerves: cord like fibers or nerves responsible for the sense of touch. Sensory nerve endings can relate the sensation of heat, cold, touch, pressure, and pain. These are found in high concentrations in the fingertips and the soles of the feet.

Sudoriferous glands: sweat glands that keep the body's temperature at normal rates. The body is regulated by the act of eliminating waste products through the pores by perspiring. Activity can increase the perspiration rates.

Fundus: base of the sweat glands with a coil shape.

Sweat pore: tube like opening in the skin that perspiration passes through.

Sebaceous: this name refers to the oil glands that secrete sebum. Sebum is useful for lubricating the skin and hair for the purpose of making them soft and silky. Sebum may harden in the pore causing pimples, or blackheads to form.

Pustule: protuberance on the skin that has a swollen base filled with pus pocket.

Scales: term given when parts of the epidermis come loose in the shedding process. An illustration of scales would be severe dandruff flakes.

Scar: faintly, elevated blotch on the skin that is evidence of an old wound or lesion that has healed.

Stain: an atypical tint that is the residue from moles, freckles or old liver spots.

Crust: an amassing of a mixture of serum, pus, and epidermal flakes that forms a scab on a sore.

Cyst: a partially solid, bump containing fluid that extends above and below the surface of the skin.

Tubercle: a protuberance which is bigger than a papule. This protuberance can be as big as a hickory nut or as small as a pea.

Vesicle: eruption filled with a clear liquid.

Elastic tissue: elastin is a substance found in the papillary layer of the dermis that gives the skin the ability to bounce back into its natural shape. Age reduces elastin found in the skin.

Lesion: a blister, scab, sore, or cyst. This occurs when an injury or disease has made a negative impact on the skin.

Excoriation: damage occurs to the skin from scratching and scraping off the shallow layers of the skin. This damage appears as a sore or an abrasion.

Fissure: damage occurs to the skin from cracks reaching to the dermis layer of the skin. This damage can appear as cracked or chapped skin.

Macule: minor, blemished mark on the skin that can be harmful or harmless depending on the cause.

Papule: risen in the skin with a solid, firm core, just above the skin's exterior surface.

Bulla: eruption on the skin full of watery fluid.

Tumor: anomalous cell mass with a wide-range of shapes, colors, and sizes. An example of a lesser tumor is a nodule.

Ulcer: open sore containing pus and loss of skin depth that appears on the skin or mucous membrane of the body.

Wheals: inflamed, irritated, itchy, uncomfortable hives appearing on the skin as a result of an allergic reaction or an insect bite.

Inflammations: condition known as dermatitis that describes the skin when it is inflamed infected, raised, or broken. This type of condition is not conducive to nail care treatments.

Eczema: unremitting, long term, skin complaint that is characterized by burning, scales, and blisters. Later stages may produce Beau Lines. These are caused by nail plate disturbances or scarring of the nail plate. Inflamed skin should not receive nail care treatments.

Fungi: 175 of the 100,000 types of fungi can exist on or in the human body, 20 of these can result in a systemic disease.

Yeasts: this is a type of fungi.

Molds: a type of fungi.

Tinea: this type of fungi is caused by an infection that has a worm like shape that works its way as the infection spreads.

Ringworm: this infection is a type of tinea.

Spores: these are the result of the formations caused by fungi; the formations have a hard exterior surface. Spores can germinate within 4 to 6 hours to spread the fungal infection when contact with the skin has been made.

Germinate: the process of take root or developing.

Chronic hyperkeratotic: a dry scaly formation on the skin that represents one of the two kinds of fungal infections that normally appears.

Pigmentation: the color of the skin that is caused by the melanin or coloring substance found present in the skin.

Chloasma: referred to as liver spots or moth spots that appear as dark spots on the face, hands, and some may appear elsewhere on the skin.

Lentigines: small brownish markings or yellowish markings referred to as freckles that can appear on the face, or other areas of the skin.

Birthmark: a nevus or that appears as a darkening spot on the skin. This spot is usually one that causes an unusual amount of pigmentation to occur in one area or it may be the result of dilated capillaries. This marking may be hereditary in nature.

Vitiligo: a particular sensitivity to the sun that is a form of leucoderma. This sensitivity affects the skin and hair. Exposure to the sun should be avoided.

Acute inflammatory: blisters, itching, cracks on any surface of the skin that represents one of the two kinds of fungal infections that normally appears on the skin. Athlete's foot is a type of acute inflammatory.

Pigmented nevus: a tumor on the skin; a mole that may have various shapes, surfaces, or color ranges.

Melanoma: a cancer that is usually serious and must be treated by a doctor.

Amelanotic melanoma: a reddish toned, moist tumor on the skin; a type of melanoma.

Herpes simplex: this viral infection occurs in the mouth and is highly contagious.

Albinism: hair, skin, and eyes are without a pigment that causes it to darken. The eyes may have pinkish tints, and the hair and skin is white.

Tan: darkening of the skin resulting from an exposure to the sun or ultraviolet rays.

Initiator: the molecule responsible for the energy boost within the polymer. This molecule touches the monomer with a charge of energy. The monomer passes the charge of energy along to another monomer by attaching itself to the next monomer, thus producing a chain of monomers or a polymer.

Matter: one of two components that everything is made from, (energy or matter). The area filled by everything that is not energy is composed of this substance.

Molecule: the simplest form or separation of a chemical into its various parts.

Monomers: the separate molecules within a polymer or chain of molecules.

Overexposure: a repeated contact with any substance that produces an allergic reaction.

Physically changed: the altering of matter from one appearance into another which can be in either a solid, liquid or gas. This altering does not change the chemical composition.

Coatings: products that shield the nail plate with a hard layer or covering.

Cross-linker: a monomer that bonds polymer chains collectively. Cross links compositions cause a more lengthier time to dissolve due to their ability to stand up to solvents.

Dermatitis: an unusual skin inflammation that can be the result of contact or allergies.

Elements: the molecules that cannot be broken down or separated from each other.

Energy: one of two components that everything is made from, (energy or matter). Light, radio waves, and microwaves are energy forms that have no substance or matter.

Evaporate: the formation of vapors that are dissolved into the air.

Gas: substance that when placed under high pressure or cooled to sub-zero temperatures that takes on a different form.

Histamines: chemicals released by the immune system to protect the body from irritations.

Solvent: any solution or substance that liquefies or softens another liquid. One example is acetone applied in the removal of nail polish. Caution should be used when using solvents to avoid the stripping of natural oils which make the nail dry and brittle. The solvent strength can be adjusted by adding 10-15% water to the solvent solution.

Ultraviolet lights (U.V): rays of light that cannot be seen. Usually light cured enhancements require the initiator molecule to have this form of energy to begin the process. These products should be placed in the dark away from heat sources in order to prevent the polymerization process from beginning in the container.

Vapor: produced when liquids evaporate into the air. Any substance that is liquid has the capacity to produce a vapor into the air, and return back into a liquid once it cools.

Polymerizations: a chemical reaction that produces or creates a polymer chain of molecules.

Polymers: a long chain of molecules which are usually in a solid form.

Primers: a substance used to increase adhesion. One example of a primer is the base coat used to improve the adhesion of a nail polish.

Saturated: the point where a solvent will become ineffective because it loses the ability to dissolve or soften the solvent. The lesser the amount of a solvent used the more likelihood of saturation.

Sensitization: the increased risk or the more a product is used then, the likelihood that overexposure can occur.

Simple polymer chains: when a lengthy chain of monomers are joined at the head and fixed to the tail to form a single chain.

Solute: name given to the substance dissolved or softened by a solvent.

Nail Technology Procedures

General Procedures

Professional, consultative technique

The professional, consultative technique involves making a good impression from the first meeting. A licensed technician needs to portray a confident, relaxed manner that conveys professionalism and knowledge to the client. This is accomplished by focusing on the client. Good eye contact and listening skills are needed at this stage. Look directly at the client when he or she is speaking. A licensed technician's tone of voice should be confident, calm, and friendly. Professionalism and knowledge is conveyed to the client by the recommendations discussed. This is an opportunity to display knowledge about skin, nails, and each type of nail service. Supportive facts and pertinent information about nail care and how that care impacts the client is important to share at this time. The good impression made at this time can mean the difference between a steady client and an unsatisfied client.

Client consultation, analysis, and recommendations

Client consultation: a conversation with the client that consists of a discussion concerning the client's general health, the health of his or her nails and skin, the client's lifestyle and needs, and the skills you can perform as a licensed technician.

Analysis: the first part of the client consultation. The skin should be examined for inflammation, infection, swelling, or broken skin. Information discussed should be noted to ensure that the client receives appropriate services and that responsible care is given in accordance with the client's general health needs.

Recommendations: The type of treatment that the client desires should be discussed. The technician is responsible for ensuring that the client knows the specifics of each treatment desired. Additionally, the client's lifestyle and needs should be taken into consideration and discussed. This discussion allows the client to make an educated decision about the service provided.

Client records

A client service record lists contact information, products, and services sold to each customer. The details of amounts charged, type of product, results obtained, the clients' preferences and signed release statements should be recorded carefully in the client service record. These records may be kept in a paper format or on the computer. These records can be useful to other nail technicians in their attempts to provide a continuity of care in your absence. Additionally, the record can include treatments that were problematic and did not achieve the desired results.

The client's file should also include the client health/record form. This form has personal information, hobbies, sport and work activities, and general health information that applies to their nail and skin care. A careful perusal of the client's file before servicing is suggested to maintain professional service.

Client health information

The client should be given a health form. The client's name, phone number, address, work, hobbies, sport activities, housework responsibilities, and nail care regime are all questions designed to gain information about the client's nail care needs. Questions about current health care conditions provide information about the client's needs, as well. It is important to learn of any known allergens and previous nail enhancements.

Clients with diabetes, arthritis, or circulatory diseases should be given treatments with precautions. Diabetics should receive their pedicures in warm, not hot water. A person with diabetes has sensitive skin and caution should be used when filing the nails back or pushing back the pterygium. The cuticles of a diabetic should never be nipped. Diabetic persons are at risk for infection, or in extreme cases, death. Persons with arthritis and circulatory diseases require gentle handling.

Healthy skin and nails

The skin and nails on the hands and feet should appear healthy through a close examination. The examination should determine that there is no inflammation, infection, swelling or broken skin. Should one of these conditions exist it is important to delicately suggest that the client see their private physician. The technician should explain carefully that to be safe that a nail treatment is not advisable at this time. The technician should be careful not to give any diagnosis of the medical condition, as this should only be given by a licensed physician. The performance of a nail treatment on skin and nails that are in poor condition could result in unnecessary pain for the client. Additionally, a nail treatment could cause legal implications for you as a licensed professional, as well as an unsatisfied customer.

Nail care treatment

Clients may ask for a particular nail care treatment. If this should happen, then the nail technician should be able to discuss the procedure desired and how it is provided, the benefits of the procedure, and the proper care and maintenance of that particular procedure. The client's lifestyle should be discussed in conjunction with the procedure and the maintenance of the procedure. One example of a lifestyle that would impact this decision is that of a gardener. It would be impractical for a gardener to have long nails. Likewise, it would be impractical for a person that plays a guitar to have their calluses removed. The discussion of how a particular nail care treatment is advisable given the client's lifestyle shows that you, as the professional are giving your client's needs the utmost consideration. This should ensure a satisfied customer relationship.

Allergic reaction

An allergic reaction can take many forms. A client's skin or nails may appear irritated after use of a certain product. This is known as a reaction and can be further evidenced by severe drying, cracking of the cuticles, onycholysis, throbbing nail beds after a fill, itching of the cuticles, and swelling around the nails. If one of these symptoms occurs, the application of the product should be stopped immediately. The health/record form should be used to make notations concerning the product and the type of reaction that occurred. This record can be referred to in the future to prevent additional allergic reactions from taking place. This can be a good consultation tool if recorded and maintained conscientiously. Likewise, the avoidance of these products on future visits should be given proper attention through documentation on the client/service record of any allergic reactions.

Client health/record form and the client service and product record

The client's records are kept in a convenient, secure location in the salon. This reference aid can be kept in the form of a hardcopy, paper format or on the computer. The record should be easily retrievable to ensure that the client is cared for appropriately.

The health/record includes three sections of information which consist of the client's general information, the client's profile and the client's medical records. The general information concerns the client's name, contact information, and preferences. The client profile includes the client's work, sports and other related activities. The medical record consists of information that helps determine safety precautions to be used in skin and nail care.

The client service and product record contains information about each visit. Services performed, retail products sold, potential nail services, and the client's targeted goals for the future.

Recommendation process

The recommendation process for the final nail care treatment is completed at the end of the client consultation. Consultation has been used to educate the client about their skin and nail care needs. The professional technician will be able to guide the client towards the correct nail treatment that fits the person's needs and lifestyle. Maintenance of the nail treatment should be discussed at this time. Clients should appreciate a custom-tailored manicure that not only solves any problems, but provides insights into their home nail care needs. Additionally, any precautions that should be taken should be reviewed before beginning the procedure. Likewise, safety gear should be worn by the nail technician and offered to the client during the procedure. The client may refuse use of the safety gear. The final result of the recommendation process should be an informed, satisfied customer.

Equipment and Supplies

Equipment

Tools are considered permanent when they do not have to be replaced on a regular basis. The manicure table usually has a storage drawer. An adjustable lamp with a 40 watt bulb is required. Larger wattages will interfere with the nail care procedures. A lower wattage will not provide enough heat for nail care procedures. Ergonomics, comfort, durability, and effortless sanitation are important factors in selecting salon chairs. Covering the seat cushion with a freshly laundered terry towel or disposable towel for each client is recommended. Sanitization can also be accomplished with a disinfectant spray applied to each seat. A plastic, metal, or glass fingerbowl is used to soak the client's fingers in warm water and antibacterial soap. The fingerbowl should be thoroughly sanitized after each client. A disinfectant container with a lid is used to immerse implements in for sanitization purposes.

The additional equipment includes manicuring cushion, sanitized wipe container, manicure oil heaters, cosmetic supply trays, electric files, nail dryer. An 8" by 12" manicuring cushion covered with a disposal towel should be used for each client. An optional cushion can be adapted from a clean, folded towel. Absorbent cotton or lint free wipes should be stored in a sanitized container with a lid. The apparatus used to heat hot oil for manicures requires a manicure oil heater. A supply tray contains polishes, polish removers, and creams. This tray requires a compact, balanced, sturdy, easy to clean exterior. The interior of the supply tray should provide an organized view of each cosmetic. The nail dryer can be used to condense the time necessary to dry the client's nails. The tool is optional. Electric files conserve time and energy in filing the nail.

Implements

Implements are the tools that must be replaced, sanitized, or disposed of after each client's appointment. Orangewood sticks are used to loosen the cuticle around the base of a nail and to clean the area underneath the free edge. This stick must be discarded or given to the client as they cannot be sanitized. Another cuticle pusher is a steel pusher. You hold the orangewood and the steel pusher as if you were holding a pencil. You can file down any rough edges on the pusher, and then you should file it down with an emery board. To shape the fee edge of hard or sculptured nails a metal file is recommended. The metal implements must be disinfected after every use. A 7"-8" nail file is required in some states. Emery boards can also be used for soft or fragile nails.

Other implements used in nail care are cuticle nipper, tweezers, nail brushes, chamois buffer, and fingernail clippers. The cuticle nipper is applied to the base of the nail to remove excess cuticle. Stringent sanitation procedures must be followed before reuse of the cuticle nippers. Tweezers are essential for removal of small particles of cuticle from the nail. Again, stringent sanitation procedures are required before reuse of the tweezers. To flatten out corrugations or wavy ridges on the nails utilize the chamois buffer. There are two kinds of chamois buffers available. The differences in these are in the closed or open handles that are available. Disposal of the chamois after each use is necessary as these cannot be sanitized. Nails are trimmed with fingernail clippers. Cutting long nails can shorten the filing time. Fingernail clippers should be sanitized after each use.

Materials used during manicures

The materials used during a manicure are disposable towels, laundered towels, cotton balls, pledgets, plastic spatula, plastic bags, trash containers, powdered alum, styptic powder, nail cosmetics, soap, polish remover, cuticle creams, cuticle oils, cuticle solvents, nail whiteners, dry nail polish, colored polishes, base coat, hardeners, top coat, liquid nail dry, hand cream, and nail conditioners. Cotton is the material recommended for use with nail polish remover. Pledgets are fiber free squares that do not stick to the nails in the same way as cotton. These squares are preferred by nail technologists. Spatulas are used to remove products from the bottles or jars. These should be replaced whenever skin contact is made. Remember to close containers tightly to prevent contamination when the product is not being used. A bag should be available near the side of the manicuring table to use for discarded materials.

Powered file

An electric or battery operated file can be used during a nail manicure. Many have the following attachments available: filing and shaping attachments, buffers, callous attachment. The filing and shaping attachments are used in the same fashion as emery boards are used. These attachments have textures that range from coarse to fine. The buffer replaces the chamois buffer. This tool is useful in leveling out corrugations and adding luster. The callous hand can achieve a smoother texture by use of the callous buffer. Sanitize each instrument before use. Disposable attachments must be discarded after use on a client. Instructor and manufacturer's guidelines must be adhered. Sensations of heat or burning can occur if an attachment is left in one place for too long of a time. Regularly check and replace instruments, as needed.

Nail Service Preparation

Three part procedure for administered services

The three part procedure requires pre-service, actual procedure, and post-service. "Pre-service" includes: sanitization of table, equipment, and implements; proper arrangement of manicuring table; antibacterial soap and hand washing; pleasant greeting; removal and safe keeping of client's jewelry; client's hand washing with antibacterial soap, followed by drying with a laundered or disposable towel; client consultation; fill out health and record form; check nails and skin for problem areas; determine whether or not service is appropriate and explain to client in consultation. Should it be determined that services are not warranted, then the nail technician should calmly explain to the client why the service cannot be performed. The nail technician may need to suggest that the client seek medical attention for the problem. Promptly note on the health and record form for future reference.

When service is determined to be appropriate then, the actual procedure will be the second part of service. The "actual procedure" includes speaking with the client during service concerning products and care suggestions; before the polish application has client make preparations for final departure (keys, adorn jewelry, put on coats or jackets). This should prevent smudges from these articles at time of departure. The third and final part of the procedure used for services is the 'post-service' which includes: scheduling client's next appointment date; include the date, time, and services on a business card or appointment card; organize workspace; follow safety and sanitation procedures to discard materials; sanitize table, equipment, implements. Sanitization of implements take about 20 minutes in the disinfectant solution; Record on client's health and record forms any pertinent information.

Pre-service sanitation

Wash implements in cool running water. Scrub tools thoroughly using soap and warm water. Soap can disrupt a disinfectants' effectiveness. Use a clean or disposable towel to dry implements. Wear gloves and use tongs to submerge implements beneath a clear disinfectant solution. Follow hand washing procedures explicitly. Rinse hands thoroughly. Dry with clean or disposable towel. Remove implements. Rinse well and dry using a clean or disposable towel. Implements should be stored according to state guidelines. Clean the manicuring table with a disinfectant. Spray table with disinfectant and let remain wet for ten minutes, wipe dry, and spray again, allow air to dry. Each client receives a clean towel placed over the manicuring cushion. Discard and restock disposable materials after each use. Give the client waterless hand sanitizer gel or wipe to use. Make a habit of washing hands in front of client.

Universal sanitation

This term is used to describe the sanitation and disinfection procedures used by salon professionals. Licensed nail technicians use universal sanitation procedures to ensure the health and safety of themselves, as well as that of their clients and employees. Training in sanitation and disinfection procedures is designed to protect the individual from harmful effects of infection or injuries. The application of professional products to the hands, feet, and nails of the client should be performed under state rules and regulations. Consequences of taking short cuts on any of these sanitation and disinfectant procedures impact the health and safety of the entire salon. Gloves, safety glasses, disinfectants, detergents, personal hygiene, sanitation and disinfectant procedures used appropriately are essential materials needed in providing a clean, safe environment. The reputation of a professional in a salon can have a positive or negative impact on the salon as a business.

Placement procedures for workspace

Organization of the nail care technician's workspace is a must. The manicure table should be sanitized thoroughly. The client's arm cushion should be wrapped with a laundered or disposable towel. Then center the cushion in the middle of the table so that the end of the towel is directed towards you. Twenty minutes prior to your first client, fill the implement sanitization container with disinfectant. Wash and dry all metal implements and place in the container. Right handed persons will want to place the sanitation container to their right. Left handed individuals should place it on their left. All cosmetics, except for the polish should go behind your disinfection container. Emery boars and chamois buffers should be placed to the right of this container for right handed technicians; to the left for left handed technicians.

The fingerbowl and brush should be centered to the left near the client. The fingerbowl bowl and the hot oil heater should stay stationary on the table. A reconditioning hot oil manicure requires the replacement of the fingerbowl and brush with the electric hot oil heater. Then, tape or fasten a plastic bag to the right side for right handed individuals and to the left side for left handed individuals. You will discard all used materials in this bag. Polishes should be staged to the left for left handed individuals and to the right for right handed individuals. The drawer should have a supply of cotton, cotton balls stored in a sealed container or bag, pumice stone or powder, a supply of chamois, instant nail dry, and any other cosmetics, or surplus supplies used regularly.

Manicure Services

Prepping the fingernail

The proper technique that should be used to apply products on the fingernail begins with the preparation of the hands and nails. A professional technique starts with the removal of dead tissue, bacteria, oil, and moisture. It is important to scrub thoroughly to prevent infection that is caused by bacteria. Fingernail infections can create problems in the nail enhancement product. These infections cause the product to lift and separate from the nail, especially infections located around the cuticle. Just as important, a nail dehydrator will assist the drying process to temporarily remove oils and moisture from the nail plate. This process lasts for about thirty minutes; performed on one hand at a time. The nail should not be overfiled because it leads to possible infections, lifting, breaking, free-edge chipping, curling of product, and an unsatisfied client.

Beginning a manicure and removing polish

If the client is right handed, then commence working on their left hand. If the client is left handed, then begin manicure on right hand. The hand not being worked on should remain soaking in the fingerbowl. Follow the 'actual procedure' guidelines and talk with the client about service and suggested products for nail care. The lists of products that you might suggest at this time are polishes, lotions, top coats, and emery boards. Start the manicure with the little finger. Saturate the cotton with nail polish remover and apply to the nails. A non-acetone remover should be applied to artificial nails. Count to ten, silently, holding saturated cotton ball on the nail with polish, before stroking the nail. To clean near the cuticle area, use an orangewood stick, cotton saturated with nail polish remover or pledgets.

Cleaning and drying the nails and applying cuticle remover

When cleansing the nails, brush the nails and hands with a sanitized nail brush. This allows the fingers to be cleansed and helps remove any unwanted fragments of cuticle from the nails. Take the hand out of the fingerbowl and brush the fingers gently with your nail brush. This application of brushing should be in a downwards motion and should begin at the first knuckle moving towards the free edge of the nails. Use a laundered or disposable towel and dry the hand thoroughly. During the drying process, you should push the cuticle back. Cuticle remover is applied with cotton tipped orangewood stick or a cotton swab. This solution should be spread liberally around the cuticles and underneath the free edge of each fingernail. The other hand remains soaking during this process.

Shaping nails and softening cuticles

To begin shaping, apply the emery board to the fingernails. Shape the nails as agreed upon during the consultation. The coarse side of the emery board works best to file the nail. File from one side to the center of the free edge and from the other side back towards the center of the free edge. Start with the little finger and work towards the thumb. Sawing is not recommended as this motion disrupts the nail plate and causes unnecessary splitting and cracking. Nails that have been soaking should not be filed as they may be too soft and have the tendency to break and split. Cut overly long nails with fingernail clippers to reduce nail filing time. When you finish filing the first hand, place the fingertips in the fingerbowl to soak. Soaking softens the cuticles.

Cleaning under the free edge and bleaching nails

The free edge of the nail is cleansed with a cotton swab or a cotton tipped orangewood stick. Remove one hand from the fingerbowl and hold the other hand over the bowl. Brush the fingernails removing all residual solvent or cuticle pits. Rest the hand on the manicure towel. Repeat the procedures for cuticle removal on the other hand. A yellow discoloration of the nail can removed with a bleaching treatment. The solution to use for bleaching should be nail bleach or a 20 volume (6%) hydrogen peroxide. The nail solution should only be applied to the nail. Use caution not to touch the client's skin or cuticle. Apply several times to remove persistent stains. Sometimes, nails require several treatments over the course of the next few appointments to get rid of the yellow discolorations.

Loosening and nipping cuticles

Cuticles are loosened by gently pushing the orangewood stick and/or spoon end of the steel pusher. If there is difficulty in pushing back the cuticle, it is important to remain gentle. An excessive amount of pressure on the base of the nail can result in damage to the matrix. Next, the cuticle is lifted off the nail. Circular movements should be applied in removing cuticles that adhere to the nail plate. The cuticle remover alleviates much of the necessity of clipping the cuticle with a nail clipper. A gentle pressure should be applied to keep from damaging parts of the nail and the nail plate. The cuticle nippers are useful to nip off any jagged excesses or hangnails. The cuticle should be removed in one piece, if possible. Wipe away any extra cuticle remover; avoid cutting into the mantle.

Applying cuticle oils and beveling the nails

Cuticle oils are applied to each individual nail. The individual nail is swabbed with cotton tipped orangewood stick or a cotton swab dipped in cuticle oil. The application of the oil should begin with the little finger and work towards the thumb. Moving in a circular fashion, apply oil and rub it into the nail. The nail is beveled underneath the free edge with an emery board. The emery board is used in an upward, even stroke. The emery board is held at a 45 degree angle against the base of the nail. Then, the stroke is applied. Uneven edges and the cuticle particles will be detached and will be removed easily. For final finishing touches, use a fine grit block buffer to remove any unwanted, additional particles from nails. The bevel nail will be smooth and even.

Buffing the nails

The nails should be buffed with the chamois buffer and dry nail polish. Use an orangewood stick in applying the dry nail polish. The buffing movement moves from the left to right with a downward stoke, and then move from the right to left with a downward stroke. This movement should be in a criss-cross pattern. Raise the back of the buffer to prevent any friction that can cause the client to feel burning. Some technicians find that spraying the hands with water reduces this heat friction caused in the buffing process. When the buffing has been completed, the client should wash thoroughly to remove any residual abrasive or dry polish from the hands. The wavy ridges or corrugated nails can be buffed smooth by using the chamois buffer. However, not every state allows the use of chamois buffers due to sanitization concerns.

Nail polish preparation

The application of nail polish commences once the client has paid for services, put on outer wear, adorned jewelry, and made preparations for departure. This ensures that the nails are not accidentally smudged during the departure. This may need to be explained to the client. Normally, the nail will receive four coatings of polish. Each bottle is prepared with a gentle roll between the palms to mix the solution. Shaking the nail polish is definitely not recommended as air bubbles may result. Air bubbles will be detrimental to the look of the professional nail treatment. Wipe off excess from the brush tip on the inside lip of the nail bottle. A small bead on the end of the nail brush is all that is required for one full swipe of the nail. Otherwise, you may get an imperfect finish to the nail.

Hand lotions and applications, oil removal, and the choice of a nail color

The pleasure of the nail care treatment is enhanced by the application of lotions and creams. Once the cuticle oils have been applied, it is beneficial to apply the lotions. Use a sanitary spatula to apply the lotion and proceed with a hand and arm massage. The hand and arm massage techniques are applicable here. Before the application of nail polish, the oils must be removed from the nail. This ensures a good adhesion to the nail. Cotton saturated in polish remover or alcohol should be used to remove all traces of oil from the nail. The client's preferences, skin tone, clothing to be worn, and seasons should be considered in the color selection. Normally, light colors will be best in the spring and summer. Dark colors are usually preferred in the fall and winter.

Finishing guidelines for nail care

The nail strengthener/ hardener are an optional finish which is applied prior to the application of a base coat. The base coat is applied to prevent the nails from being stained. The base coat also assists in the adhesion process. The colored polish should be applied twice; however it is important to do both hands before beginning the second coat of colored polish. Use a cotton tipped orangewood stick saturated with nail polish remover or a flat nylon 6-8 bristle brush to keep the cuticle clear of nail polish. This brush should not be left to sit in the nail polish remover as this can cause damage to the bristles. The polish corrector pen is not recommended due to its unsanitary nature. The top coat prevents flaking or chipping. Instant nail dry is an optional treatment used to shorten drying time, enhances the shine, and prevents splotches.

Nail polish application

The four coats applied in the nail polish application include: the base coat, two coats of color, and the top coat. The base coat is applied first, with the top coat going on last. As with all the other coatings, the procedure for holding the brush is critical. Hold the brush at 30-35 degree angle approximately 1/16 inches away from the cuticle. The brushing is set in motion at the center of the nail. Brush away from the cuticle, towards the edge of the nail. If an area of the nail is missed in the swipe, then swipe again. Do not dab at the spots as this creates an uneven look to the nail's final appearance. The application of thin, even coats create a more attractive look. The thinner applications add durability to the treatment as it bonds better, than a thicker, single coating.

French and American manicures

French and American designs allow the technician to be creative with hand painted art, air-brushing, rhinestones, pearls, or stripping tape. The American manicure will have a more subdued white polish; while French manicures use a striking white on the free edge of the nail. In a French manicure, the base coat is self-leveling. This coat will assist in an even appearance, covering up defects. White polish is applied in a diagonal line. There should be a 'v' on the free edge of the nail. This 'v' line may also be filled in with polish. Apply a white coat underneath the free edge. Allow to dry. A translucent white, pink, natural or peach polish is applied; follow with a top coat over the nail and free edge; the free edge should be treated similar to polishes previously applied.

Polish applications

The five kinds of polish applications include: full coverage, free edge, hairline tip, slimline or free walls, and half moon or lunula. Full coverage of the nail is accomplished when the nail has been completely coated with polish. The free edge application refers to the free edge in an unpolished state; to forestall the flaking or chipping of the polish. Likewise, the hairline tip refers to the nail plate polished with the removal of 1/16 inch of polish from the free edge. In order to make the nail appear thin and slender, it is advisable to use a slimline or free wall application. This application allows for a 1/16 inch margin on each side of the nail. The half moon shape or lunula application calls for the base of the nail to be unpolished. This unpolished portion forms a half moon shape.

Reconditioning hot oil manicures

<u>Pre-service procedures</u>

Pre-service procedures include: table arrangement, heater preparations, preheating the lotions, greetings, hand washing, and client consultation. The table arrangement includes the regular manicure set up procedures with the addition of the hot oil heater, the plastic cup, and lotions. Fill the plastic, disposable cup with hand lotion. Place it into the heater. Then, allow the lotion 10-15 minutes for pre-heating. This should be done prior to seating the client for the manicure. When you do invite your client to the manicure table, remember to smile. Instruct the client to remove jewelry, and to wash their hands with antibacterial soap. You should also wash your hands at this time. Begin a client consultation. In the consultation, you will have learned whether your client is dominantly right handed or left handed. Begin with the client's less dominant or less preferred hand.

<u>Benefits and supplies</u>

Uneven, brittle nails and dry, damaged cuticles require special care. One way to improve these conditions is through a reconditioning hot oil manicure. This process should be performed on a weekly basis for maximum benefit. The client will receive beneficial care that softens the skin. Persons with a nail biting habit may find that this treatment keeps rough cuticles soft. The supplies needed for a reconditioning hot oil manicure include: hot oil heater, plastic cups, and oil for the heater. The hot oil heater is an electric appliance. This appliance is used to warm solutions. The plastic cup is placed into the heater after it has been filled with the desired lotion, cream, or oil. Olive oil, or hand lotion can be used, although there are commercially prepared products available. Reconditioning hot oil manicure requires professionalism and product knowledge.

<u>Steps</u>

Reconditioning warm oil manicures begin with the removal of the old nail polish. Next, shape the nails on the less preferred hand. Third, the fingertips of the preferred hand should be resting in warm lotion. Simultaneously, the other hand should be filed. Fourth, distribute lotion by spreading the lotion on the hand to the elbow on each arm. Use a spatula to dip more lotion from the heated container when necessary. Fifth, once enough lotion has been applied, the hand and arm message should be given. Sixth, the orangewood stick enclosed with cotton is used to push the cuticles back. Seventh, if your state allows, then use the nippers to trim off the remaining cuticle. Rest their hand on a laundered or disposable towel. At the eighth stage, repeat procedures for steps 5-7 on other hand.

The ninth step is the point in which the client needs to rewash their hands to remove any extra lotion. If re-washing is not warranted, then use a warm terry-clothed towel to remove the extra lotion. In step ten, the pores on the arm and hand need to be closed. Wrap the arm in the cold towel. The pores are closed with the application of the cold towel and gentle pressure. In step eleven, saturate cotton with alcohol or nail polish remover. Wipe off excess oil from fingernails. Begin application of the nail polish in step twelve. The manicure post-service is completed in step thirteen. The plastic cup from the hot oil heater is disposed of at this stage. Approved sanitization products should be used in step fourteen to clean the heater for use by the next client.

Manicure of male clients

In a male client's manicure the colored polish is replaced with a clear polish or a buffing cream. The male client should be greeted with a handshake. Consultation includes: type of service requesting, client information form, evaluation of nails, and product recommendations. The manicure begins with removal of old polish, and nail shaping. The nail shape should be the same as agreed upon in consultation. Most men prefer a round shape. Areas that may require more work on males include the cuticles. The cuticles will require softening. Wash and dry nails and hands thoroughly. Next, either buff the nails or go on to the hand lotion and massage. Use of a citrus or spice scent is advisable. If called for, apply a base coat, a clear satin topcoat, followed by instant nail dry in a clear nail polish.

Spa manicures

The spa manicure includes a massage accompanied by a form of exfoliation. This business is rapidly becoming lucrative and exclusively services many clients. The professional trained to provide this service will find it to be rewarding. The technician should be able to provide a thorough nail and skin analysis. Distinctive names have been given to a variety of spa treatments. For instance, "The Rose Garden Rejuvenation Manicure" refers to a manicure featuring the use of hydrating rose oils and rose petals. Another example is found in "Alpha Hydroxy Acid Manicure". This one features the use of an alpha hydroxy acid commodity used primarily for skin exfoliation and rejuvenation. Aromatic paraffin cups, aromatherapy, aromatic hand and arm lotions used in combination with hand and arm massages, reflexology, hand masks, and temperate, damp towel applications enhance the experience of the spa manicure.

Paraffin wax treatment

A paraffin wax treatment is given to the client after the consultation and review of any existing previous health and record forms. Use antibacterial liquid soap to cleanse your hands thoroughly. Then, the client should place his or her jewelry in a safe location. The client will be instructed to roll up long sleeves, cleanse his or her hands thoroughly, and to completely dry his hands. If any cuts, wounds, disorders, or diseases are found, discontinue the service. Use an antiseptic spray, followed by a moisturizing lotion. Test the wax paraffin temperature. Then, align the palm flat with the wrist slightly bent and fingers separated. Assist the client in dipping in one hand up to the wrist for a period of approximately 3 seconds. Allow cooling and solidifying of the paraffin once the hand has been removed from the wax.

<u>Benefits and cautions</u>

The paraffin wax treatment is used for therapeutic and pleasurable benefits. Heat and moisture are trapped beneath the skin by the paraffin wax. Then, the pores of the skin open and blood circulation improves. Dry skin is rejuvenated. The petroleum by-product, paraffin, is purchased as a solid wax that can be melted into a liquid. This liquid must remain at 125-130 degrees Fahrenheit to be used in the treatment. Special heating appliances are used for just this purpose. A properly prepared paraffin wax treatment will not harm artificial nails, wraps, tips, gels, artificial nail embellishments, or natural nails. State guidelines should be adhered in providing this service to a client. A note of caution is warranted in giving this service to person's who suffer with poor circulation, skin irritations, cuts, burns, rashes, warts, eczema, swollen veins, or the elderly.

<u>Procedures</u>

The procedures to include a pre-sanitation and consultation are the same as discussed previously. The client should be a part of the decision process regarding the manicure selection having discussed the client's nail care needs. Old polish should be removed from the nail. Shape the nails into the selected, preferred shape. Repair the nails using proper techniques and procedures. Gently rub moisturizers into the client's hands. Follow the steps for a paraffin wax treatment at this stage. The manicure procedure will begin once both hands have received the treatment. The manicure should begin at the stage of the 'actual procedure'. Actual procedure for the manicure includes a discussion on the maintenance of the hand and nail care. The 'post service' stage of the nail care is carried on until completion.

The final procedures for a paraffin wax treatment allow for several applications of the hand in the wax paraffin. Once, the first application has cooled, dip hand at least 3-5 times more. Then use plastic wrap to cover the hands completely. Have the client adorn a cloth mitt over the plastic wrap. Continue the paraffin wax treatment process with the other hand. The paraffin should remain on the hands for a period of time lasting about 10-15 minutes. The paraffin is then removed. Massaging gently will allow the wax to loosen. Begin the massage at the wrist and work downwards. The paraffin should peel easily from the hands. Discard the used paraffin using proper disposal techniques. The paraffin wax treatment should give the hands a moisturized, softened complexion. The treated hands are now ready for the manicuring procedure to commence.

Pedicure Services

Pre-service procedures

The pre-service pedicure is the first of the three parts of a pedicure. Pre-service includes the strict adherence to procedures for sanitization. The stations will have available a pedicuring stool, client's chair, and a foot rest for the client. One laundered, terry cloth towel will be placed on the floor in front of the client's chair. The client will need this towel to place his or her feet upon during the pedicure service. Another laundered towel used for drying should be placed over the footrest. The standard manicuring table will be laid out on the surface of the pedicure table. Additionally, you need toe separators, foot cream, foot files, toenail clippers, antiseptic foot spray, foot cream, foot powder, and pedicure slippers. The pedicure basin should be filled with warm water and liquid soap. Cheerfully greet the client. Complete the client consultation.

Pedicure service

Pedicure service requires timely, efficient service. This involves knowledge of products being used, as well as organization. The organization of implements, products, and supplies will go a long way in proving to the client that you are a professional in your field. Next, try to limit distractions. Follow your client's wishes and body language in determining the levels of chattiness that you use. Some client's may wish to doze off at this stage. They should be provided the opportunity to do so if they so wish. The mild, touch on the foot that tickles is not recommended. Rather, a gentle firm compelling touch or grip is sought. Usually, this is accomplished by gripping the foot between the thumb and the midtarsal area of the fingers; locking the foot in place. This should overcome any touchiness or tickling feet sensations that can make a pedicure uncomfortable.

The thumb or index finger should be positioned on the ball of the foot; usually, located at the beginning of the foot's longitudinal arch. Some pressure applied on this spot can reduce tension. Actual performance of the pedicure is sub-divided into five basic steps: soaking, nail care, skin care, massage, and nail polishing. Each client may have different levels of nail care in place within their regiment. Therefore, if a client comes in requiring only nail care, then by all means start at that point. The nail care step should require 15 minutes of the client's time, however, if other steps are completed a longer length of time will be required. The massage technique may be favored and will add to the overall pleasure for the client if performed correctly. This also has the ability to reduce the stress and the tension.

Steps in performing a pedicure

In step one, shoes and socks are removed. If the client has on long pants, then the cuffs need to be rolled. In step two, the feet need to be sprayed or wiped with an antiseptic. In step three, the client soaks his or her feet in the soap bath for 5-10 minutes. In step four, the client's toes are dried; special attention is placed to the area between the toes. Then, the client places both feet on the towel. In step five, the nail polish is removed. In step six, the nails are trimmed evenly with the toe. In step seven, the toe separators are positioned between each toe. In step eight, the nails are filed with an emery board. Filing consists of filing directly across the nail with a curve at each corner.

In step nine, the foot is filed on the ball of the foot and on the heel of the foot. This filing removes dry skin and calluses from the foot. This should not be performed to the point of irritation or blood. In step ten, the foot is rinsed in the bath after the toe separators have been removed from the toes. In step 11, steps nine and ten are repeated on the other foot. In step 12, the right foot toe nails are brushed with the nail brush. Dry the foot. When this is completed, replace the toe separators. In step 13, cuticle solvent should be applied with cotton tipped orangewood stick. Start at the little toe and work towards the big toe. Solvent applied under the free edge will soften excess skin for removal.

In step 14, push cuticles back with an orangewood stick or metal pusher. According to state regulations, use the cuticle nippers. Remove hangnails as needed. In step 15, remove the toe separators from the toes. Then, have the client dip the foot into the bath. Have the client to raise foot just over the bath. Next, use the nail brush on the foot to detach any residual cuticle or solvent from the foot. Dry thoroughly and position the foot on the towel. In step 16, lotion the foot. In step 17, use foot massage techniques on left foot. In step 18, repeat steps 12-17 on right foot. In steps, 19 remove lotion with cotton saturated with nail polish remover. Step 20, use toe separators and polish toes. In step 21, powder the client's dry feet.

Pedicure post-service procedures

Pedicure post service procedures require that you schedule another pedicure engagement for your client. The client should receive advice regarding their foot care needs. Reminders concerning foot wear are appropriate, at this time. The client should be encouraged to buy the recommended commodities to ensure that the client has the proper polishes, foot creams, or top coats needed. This will go a long way in maintaining the client's pedicure. The pedicure basin should be emptied and sanitized with a hospital grade disinfectant. Likewise, the area should be disinfected. This includes sanitization of the table and the foot stool area. Used materials should be discarded. A new trash bag may be required. Pre-service sanitation should be performed for approximately 20 minutes as regulated by the state; otherwise check your state's guidelines. The table should be returned to a basic set up for further service needs.

Scrubs

Scrubs can flatten smooth the skin on feet that is dried out, peeling, or callused. The scrub can also be used in the removal of this damaged skin. The abrasions in the scrub should be balanced out by the alpha hydroxy acids or oils. This will allow the skin to be softened without causing harm to the skin. The exfoliating agent is the abrasion within the scrub. The abrasive will cause the dead tissue on the foot to dislodge. Some exfoliating agents include: Sea sand, ground apricot kennels, pumice, quartz crystals, and plastic beads. Glycerin is also an agent found in pedicure scrubs. The exfoliating agent acts as a binder with the peeling tissue. In turn, the peeling tissues pull away from the living tissues existing beneath the dead tissues. Scrub pedicures also contain a variety of vitamins, essential aroma oils, and moisturizers.

Soaks

The term soaks refers to products used by a technician in a pedicure bath. This bath is useful for softening and sanitizing the foot. Moisturizers provide hydration to the foot. Surface-active substances present in the soaks provide a deeper penetration of the active ingredients within the product. One example of this type of surface-active agent is Dead Sea salts. Dead Sea salts contain potassium, magnesium, calcium, and sodium. These minerals are key elements in therapeutic quality of the soaks. Soaks also include antioxidants which are useful in balancing out the effects of the surfactants. This balance is important in maintaining the skin's health. One natural antiseptic is tree oil. Aromas are an important element in aromatherapy. There are a number of bath soaks to choose from, however, bath soaks should be selected to best fit the client's needs.

Add-on products

Products used to promote the experience of a pedicure are kept on hand by skilled technicians. Some of the more callused feet may require an application of a strong, concentrate of callus softeners. Use of a 20 percent alpha hydroxy acid preparation will cause the skin to be soft enough for easy removal of the hardened callus build ups. Mineral clays, sea extracts, hydrating alpha hydroxy acids, aromatherapy oils, and skin softeners are all products used in the creation of a "mud facial" for the feet. Use of "mud facials" can add a luxurious, enjoyable aspect to the pedicure experience. Hot paraffin baths increase blood flow and reduces inflammations caused by arthritis or joint pain. Hot paraffin wax treatments should not be applied to persons with poor circulation problems or diabetic conditions. Other products include pedicure disposable or foam slippers, or sandals.

Massage preparations and massage oils

Massage oils are selected based on the quality of the product. If the massage oil is absorbed into the skin too quickly, then the oil is not of good quality. However, this can be determined by the molecular size of the oil. Large molecule oils are lanolin and mineral oil. Blends of therapeutic oils include jojoba oil and vitamin E oil. Some oils are selected for their aromas. Such oils are used in aromatherapy. Tea tree oil is used for applications requiring antiseptic and antifungal benefits. Some massage oils are combined into a personalized composition by the technician. Base massage oil, essential oils, and aromatherapy oils are formulated into a composition that the technician selects. This composition should be customized to meet the needs of the client. Massage lotions are absorbed more quickly and are used as the final touch to the massage.

Diamond nail file and foot paddles

The diamond nail file is useful for filing or thinning the free edge of toenails. The file is made from a metallic and diamond mixture. This file can be purchased in coarse, medium, or fine grits. Coarse grits are preferred for use on the toenails. This file can be sanitized for reuse. The file should be sanitized in a disinfectant solution. The mixture of the metallic and the diamond compounds add durability to this instrument. Therefore, the cost is warranted. The foot files or paddles can be purchased in a wide assortment of grits. The file that is most economical for purchase is the one that can be sanitized in a disinfectant solution. The foot paddle has individual parts that can be sanitized. However, the abrasive surface component is disposable and must be replaced after a few disinfectant cycles.

Toenail nippers, curette, and nail rasp

Toenail nippers are used for professional trimming of the toenail. They do not resemble store bought toenail clippers. The jaws of the nipper can be bowed or straight; with a pointed or blunt end. The pointed ends make the trimming of a plicatured nail more effective. The nail trimmed correctly prevents the growth of an ingrown toenail. The curette is used to clean out the debris from underneath the nail boundaries. The experienced nail technician will be able to feel uneven surfaces with the use of the curette. Usually, it is the big toe that requires use of the curette. A double ended curette has a 1.5mm diameter on one end and a 2.5mm diameter on the other end is the preferred tool. The nail rasp is a metallic file used in cutting or filing in a single direction.

Water baths

Water baths consisting of vibrators and water heaters are used by the nail technician. These can be portable or stabilized customized built types. The chair that the client sits in for this treatment should allow maximum comfort in a semi to private area. The chair positioned on a platform is best for the nail technician's posture. Some whirlpools are portable for ease of water filling and draining. However, there is some specifically plumbed in water basins with hot and cold running water attached. These can have drains for easy use, too. Whatever the variety of water bath used it is essential that the equipment be sanitized and disinfected after each client's use. The technician should be cognizant of posture and comfort for both herself and her client. This awareness will include the selection of a pedicurist stool and chair which can be adjusted.

Cuticle nippers, files, and pedicure carts

Cuticle nippers are used on the hands and the feet. The name is misleading as the cuticle nipper is not used to cut living tissue. Instead, it is used to cut away small particles from the nail corner in the lesser toes. These are the toes numbered two through five on the foot. This tool is especially helpful in cutting the minor toenails on the little toes. The electric file is best used on thick, abnormally formed toenails. Files are purchased in hand held varieties, cable driven varieties, belt driven varieties, or in micromotor varieties. This tool should be used with caution and practice as it can cause damage when used improperly. The nail technician sits on the pedicure cart. This compact stool on wheels can have a foot rest, drawers, shelves, and even a place for foot baths.

Pedicure procedures

Full service pedicure begins with soak set to approximately 104 degrees Fahrenheit; some clients with compromised circulation require temperatures of 100 degrees Fahrenheit. Soaking solutions comes with a manufacturer's recommendation that should be followed. The foot should be soaked for a period of 5 minutes to ensure softening and sanitization has taken place. Double-check that your supplies, materials, instruments, and equipment needs are within easy reach. In step two, you will need to remove old nail polish from one foot, while the other foot soaks. Callus and cuticle softeners will also need to be applied. Use the curette to remove debris from the margin of the toe. Trim toenails with nail nippers. Next, use the curette. Use the nail rasp or the diamond file or electric files to smooth and shape the nail. Repeat on other foot.

The third step of the pedicure procedure begins with skin softening in the soaking solution. The scrub is used to exfoliate one foot at a time. The scrub should be generously rubbed on the skin. The pedicurist should scrub any dry, peeling skin from the exterior of the foot with the use of a massaging technique. A moderate scrubbing motion will allow friction to build up that is essential in removing the buildup present on the heel of the foot. The foot paddle should be used. Do not remove all of the callus material as this will make your client sore. Rinse the foot, cleaning between the toes. This should be accompanied by a discussion of the foot products that you recommend. Apply a mask if necessary. Then, wrap the foot in a laundered towel and allow to rest. The continued procedures for step three require the redirection of your attention to the other foot. The mask product can be left on the wrapped foot for approximately 5-10 minutes. Repeat the third step procedures on the unwrapped foot. Finally, a hot wax service can be applied. This can be applied in conjunction with the mask or as a standalone feature. Once, the wax has been applied this foot is wrapped in a plastic bag and covered with a terry cloth boot or wrapped in a laundered towel. Repeat steps with other foot. The client is given a period of 5-10 minutes for relaxation and treatment purposes. In step 4 the massage technique is applied to the feet. The massage is beneficial in the promotion of good circulation and reduces muscle tension in the feet.

The full service pedicure step 5 is optional as not everyone desires application of nail polish. However, if the client chooses this step, then the nail technician should place toe separators on the foot. Massage lotion will require removal with a nail polish remover. Then, the application should begin with a base coat, followed by two color coats of polish. The final coat is a topcoat. Allow the feet to rest on the towel to dry. In step 6, the client should be advised as to nail care and the products recommended for use at home. Give the client the opportunity to talk about the service just received. Record on the client health record forms after client leaves the salon. Set the next appointment before client's departure. Sanitize and disinfectant thoroughly. Make preparations for next client.

Massage

Hand and arm massages

Hand and arm massages are pleasurable and therapeutic to the client. As such, the massage can be a great motivator for the client in receiving services. The massage is normally performed just prior to the nail polish application portion of the manicure. The massage and its oils will provide beneficial effects to the skin; however, it is mandatory that the oil be removed from the nail before further applications of nail care products. The nail plate must be cleansed from any trace of oil, cream, wax, or lotions to ensure proper adhesion of nail products. These can be easily removed with the use of alcohol or nail polish removers. The massage is optional in basic manicures; however, the addition of a massage to the basic manicure could ensure a more satisfied client that is more likely to return for future services.

Hand massage techniques

Hand massage techniques include the relaxer movement or joint movement, and the joint movement on the fingers. The hand massage initiates after the application of lotion or creams. The client's elbow should rest on a cushion covered with a laundered towel. Brace the client's arm with your hand, then with your other hand, bend and hold the client's wrist back and forth in a slow movement. Do this repeatedly for about 5-10 cycles. You should feel the client's muscles relax. The joint movement on the fingers is conducted with the client's arm down. Use your left hand to brace the client's arm. Massage with your right hand, beginning at the little finger of the client's left hand. Hold the base of nail gently and gently rotate the finger about 3-5 times to form a circular pattern.

The final hand massage technique includes the circular movement on the back of the hand and fingers. Use your thumbs to rotate the entire back of the client's hand. Begin rotation at the little finger and go along towards the thumb. Gently apply pressure at the tips of the fingers. Return to the ringer finger and index finger, squeezing gently. Then, go back to the middle finger and squeeze at the tip of the finger. This pressure on the fingertips provides a restoration effect to the normal blood flow cycle. Caution must be used in the application of massages to people with high blood pressure, heart conditions, arthritis, or history of strokes. The massage intensifies the circulation and may cause unintended results. The client suffering from the previous health concerns should gain permission from their physician before receiving massage services.

The additional hand massage techniques include the circular movement in the palm and the circular movement on the wrists. The circular movement in the palm or the effleurage begins with a light relaxing, rub. The client's elbow rests on the cushion while your thumbs are used to create a circular rotation movement. Each thumb should be rotating in the opposite direction of each other. The circular movement on the wrist begins with the hand of the client resting in both of your hands. Your thumbs will be positioned on top of the client's hands and your fingers will support underneath the client's hand. Again, rotate your thumbs in oppositional directions up and down from the knuckles to the wrist. Lastly, gently twist the client's wrist in opposite directions to give a frictional, invigorating massage.

Arm massage techniques

Wringing movements and kneading movements: The wringing movements of the arm provide a friction massage. Friction massage is a term used for a deep rubbing massage applied to the muscles. The client's elbow should be bent. The arm should be positioned in front. The palm of the hand is resting down. Begin at the wrist and work towards the elbow, applying a gentle twisting movement with your fingers of both hands. Begin twisting in opposite directions in the same manner as you would wring water out of a wash rag. The kneading massage is also called petrissage kneading. This manipulation is used to stimulate the blood flow. Position your thumbs horizontally across the top side of the client's arm. Squeeze and gently twist in opposite directions. This kneading allows the fleshy tissue to move over the bone and invigorates the muscles in the arm.

Cream or lotion distribution and effleurage: The distribution of cream or lotion is simply the act of placing a little lotion or cream on the arm. This lotion or cream is massaged into the arm beginning at the wrist and working towards the elbow. More cream may need to be applied, if the arm is dry. In the effleurage, the client should rest their arm on the table and you should brace the arm with your hands. Fingers rest under the clients and your thumbs are used to provide an oppositional rotation from the wrist to the elbow. Begin with palm side up. At the elbow, your hand moves to cup the elbow, sliding down the length of the arm to the wrist. Then repeat the entire cycle 3-5 times over. Turn the client's arm over and repeat procedure on opposite side of arm.

Friction massage

The friction massage is presented during the rotation of the elbow technique. The rotation of the elbow massage is accomplished by bracing the client's arm with your left hand. This is followed by a cream application on the client's elbow. The cream is applied with cotton tipped orangewood stick. The elbow should be held by your right hand. Rotate your hand over the elbow 3-5 times using a gentle rub. Finally, position your left arm towards the top of the client's forearm. Slide both of hands downward from the forearm to the elbow towards the fingertips. This slide movement should be similar to the same movements in using to climb down a rope. This should be repeated over the course of 3 or 5 times. This should complete the arm massage techniques. The client is ready for further servicing.

Foot massage

Foot massage includes three forms of hand manipulation: effleurage, petrissage, and tapotement. The first technique involves the relaxer movement to the joints of the foot. The client's foot lays on the footrest or stool. Meanwhile, you grasp the leg above the ankle with your left hand; bracing the foot and leg. Then, position your hand just under the toes and rotate the foot in a circular motion. The second technique involves the effleurage on top of the foot. Both thumbs are positioned on top of the instep. Using a counter clock movement, move your thumbs downwards towards the center of the top of the foot down towards the toes. Slide the hand back along the instep and repeat 3-5 times. This relaxation technique has additional therapeutic benefits.

The third technique involves the effleurage on the bottom of the foot. The counter clockwise movement begins at the ball of the heel. Then, slide the hands back to the top of foot for maximization of the relaxation. The effleurage movement on the toes begins at the smallest toe and moves towards the big toe. The thumb is placed on top; the index is positioned on the bottom of the foot. Each individual toe is rotated in a circular movement. In the fifth technique, the joint movement is replaced with a figure eight instead of a circular motion. This provides a benefit of a soothing, relaxing massage. The joint movement should be repeated 3 to 5 times on each toe for maximum benefit.

<u>Fist twist compression, effleurage on the instep, and percussion movement</u>

The fist twist compression involves the right hand formed into a fist. The left hand administers a measured pressure onto the foot. The right hand twists around under the foot for a cycle of about 3-5 times. This also improves blood circulation. The effleurage on the instep should be accomplished by placement of the fingers on the ball or heel of the foot. The finger movements are in a clockwise and counter clockwise pattern. The foot should be massage from the ball of the foot to the end of each toe. At the end of each toe give the tip of the toe a mild squeeze. The percussion movement is formed by a light chopping movement over the whole foot that reduces blood flow. This is the final step in the massage of the foot.

Thumb compression and the metatarsal scissors

The technique used for the thumb compression or friction movement is made by balling up your fist leaving the thumb extended. Then, pressure is applied with the thumb as you move your fist towards the ball of the heel. Examine the bottom of the foot for nodules or bumps. You will want to be extremely careful as sore spots may be present. This examination allows you to show a consideration of your client's well being. This manipulation will allow improve circulation. The metatarsal scissors or a petrissage massage that is directed along the metatarsal bones. The thumb is positioned under the foot; the fingers are placed on top of the foot. A measured, consistent pressure should be applied with the thumb and lower fingers to increase the blood flow to the foot. This manipulation continues for a period of 3-5 cycles.

Electric filing

Types of bits

The types of bits used on the nail are natural nail bits, sanding bands, diamond bits, carbide bits, backfill bits, buffing bits, abrasive stone bits, pedicure bits, and jewelry bits. The natural nail bit is made from a synthetic rubber. This bit is best used for polishing jewelry, for the removal of pterygium on natural nails, for smoothing out ridges within the natural nail, and for creating a very shiny appearance on the nail. The sanding band is comprised of a circular, paper file that can be slipped onto the mandrel. The sanding band is appropriate for use in sanding artificial nails. Diamond bits consist of metallic and diamond substances. They can be purchased in extra fine, fine, medium and coarse grits. These bits should have an even distribution of diamond particles to ensure quality.

The carbide bit can be purchased in extra fine, fine, medium and coarse grits. The coarser, deeper cuts are the result of larger carbide bits. Bits that cut in two directions are called crosscut bits. These are better than one sided; right sided cuts. Backfill bits are available in a wide assortment and should be purchased when a shorter, smaller barrel bit is needed. Buffing bits are made from organic substances such as chamois, leather, goat's hair brushes, or cotton rag wheels. These disposable bits are used in conjunction with buffing cream. Non-concentric, abrasive stone bits are white, pink, lavender, or blue ceramic stones. They are not to be used. Pedicure bits are diamond bits used to remove calluses and to thin toenails. Carbide bits known as jewelry bit are used to fasten nail jewelry.

Use of electric file

Support your hand on the table. Hold the handle of the drill jus as if you were writing. Your other hand should be positioned so that the wrist is resting on the table. The pinky finger of both hands should be touching. This will allow the negative pressure to be deflected from the tip of the bit and give you a more professional hold on the instrument. Electric file bits should be positioned flat to the nail. It is incorrect to use a right angle position. Rings of fire or ridges should be avoided as they are the result of the bit touching the cuticle area at the wrong angle. The nail should be allowed to cool as the technician works from right to left. At the end of each direction, the bit is lifted off. The nail should not get hot.

The speed of the file will be determined by the technician. However, these are some conditions that should be avoided with excessive speed: the bit jerks the nail and rotates around the finger; the drill makes a squealing sound; or the client complains of heat sensations. Slow speeds may cause the drill to stall or to jam up. The natural nail should only be prepared with the use of the synthetic natural bit made for this purpose. An artificial nail will require occasional maintenance. This is achieved by a bullet or cone used for application of a fill. The use of this bit will need to be used cautiously so as not to cause damage to the natural nail. Cuticles are prepped with a cone or flat tipped cone bit. Work from right to left; bringing the finger towards the bit.

Lifted product and cracks

The sharp edge of a barrel bit referred to as the French backfill bit is useful for lifting damaged ends. Use the sharp edge and cut a trench into the lifting just under the area where the lifting stops. Approximately 75% of the lifting will need to be cut away. The lifted piece of product can be bent and broken off cleanly. The remainder of the lifting should be beveled off even with the natural nail. This allows the lifted product to be removed without replacing the entire application of the product. In the instances of cracking, the slender barrel, bullet bit is used. This bit is used to bevel a wide trench to expose the crack. This should be done slowly and carefully as the exposure of the crack is revealed. This procedure allows the crack to be repaired quickly.

Finishing and buffing oils

Finishing refers to changing out of bit grits as you work. Graduate or change out your bit grits to give your pedicure a smooth, even texture. The pressure applied should be lighter as you move on to the use of finer bits. The shaping of the perimeter nails should never be done with an electric bit. This should be accomplished with a hand file. A fine bit or a buffer bit is useful for filing over edges of the nail and in making sure that the nails have a complete, smooth, even finish. For a high shine buffing, use cotton rag wheels, chamois, or leather. Use a light pressure as these materials can tend to heat up. Buffing creams contain pumice and are useful in the buffing process. Use the goat's hair brush for application of the buffing cream. Follow by a buffer bit.

Nail Enhancement

Backfill

Backfills use an assortment of bits. Use a barrel tip for thinning the free edge of the nail. Sometimes, you will want to use white tip powder to create smile lines. The smile line can be drawn first with a pencil. Then, the three cuts follow: one cut from the right groove wall, one cut along the center, and one along the center to the left groove wall. Then, you will position the nail in such a way as to allow visibility of the profile of the nail. 75% of the acrylic can now be removed. The application of the white tip powder will need to remain the same density in each nail. Do not overlap the white tip powder on the new smile line recently cut. Remove excess. Allow the white powder to dry before application of pink or clear product.

Nail tip application pre-service procedures

The nail tip application pre-service procedure begins with thorough sanitization methods. The standard set up of the manicuring table should include: abrasives, buffer blocks, nail adhesives, and nail tips. The client should be greeted with a smile. Then, the client should be instructed to wash his or her hands with an antibacterial soap. The hands should be dried with a laundered or disposable towel. The client consultation should begin with an examination of previous history of the client record/health form. Any additional information should be noted. The nails should be thoroughly examined before proceeding with any nail care services. Subtlety should be used if there is a need to refuse services. Likewise, the client with obvious medical conditions should gently be urged to seek medical attention. The reason for refusal of services should also be noted on the client's record/ health forms.

Nail tip application procedures

In step 1, the nail tip application begins with the removal of old nail polish. The nail polish is removed working from the little finger towards the thumb. In step 2, the cuticle is pushed back with mild, pressure applied to the cuticle with a cotton tipped orangewood stick or sanitizable cuticle pusher. In step 3, the nail plate is shined with a medium or fine abrasive. This is done to remove the nail's shine and to remove natural oils from the nail. In step 4, the nail tips are selected. The nail tips are the right size if they completely cover the nail plate from side to side. They should not cover more than 50% of the natural nail's surface. Pre-bevel the nail tip before application. This reduces filing times later on in the manicure.

The nail tip application procedure from step 5 includes a nail antiseptic dehydrating spray. This antiseptic dehydrating solution can also be applied on the end of cotton tipped orangewood sticks. This solution allows the nail to dehydrate and creates a better adhesive surface. In step 6, an adhesive substance is used to secure the tip of the artificial nail to the natural nail. The glue is applied from the middle of the natural nail to its free edge. In step 7, the procedure to slide on the nail is to pause at the point of the free edge. At this point, you will hold the at a 45 degree angle. Then, you sway the tip back and forth until you have positioned it into the correct spot. Remain still for 5-10 seconds to secure the drying process.

In step 8, you put on a string of droplets of adhesive between the nail plate and the tip of the artificial nail. This creates a seamless bond that gives strength between the nail and the artificial tip. In step 9, use a pair of tip cutters or a pair of large sized nail clippers for cutting the nail tip to the proper length. Begin cutting from one side and work towards the other side. This technique should prevent any failing of the nail tip. In step 10, use medium coarse abrasives for sanding the nail. This should remove the shine. This allows the blending of the two to look natural. The proper technique is to hold the file flat against the nail. Angle filing is not recommended as it creates damaging grooves within the nails' surface.

The nail tip application procedure in step 11 consists of buffing the natural nail plate and the artificial nail tip. This buffing creates a blended appearance and removes the delineating line between the two surfaces. In step 12, an abrasive is applied in shaping the longer nails. In step 13, the tip application has been finished. The blended application of the artificial nail tip has melded with the natural nail. Now, the time has come to apply an additional nail service as previously requested by the client during the consultation. This application of an additional service can be in the form of a wrap, acrylic nails, or gel nails. However, some clients may prefer a temporary service and need only a drop of cuticle oil on each nail. The oil is then buffed to create a shine.

Alternative tip applications

The alternative tip applications refer to the tip well cutting techniques. These techniques are recently established in an effort to create the smile lines with white tips or with traditional tips. This is accomplished without blending. The tips of the nails need to be sized for fit. The tip cutter is positioned on a slant, careful not to angle the instrument. The well will be removed if you cut swiftly and uniformly. Then, finish off by filing smooth. Use a minimum of acetone to wipe the edge of the smile line to allow for the finishing touches to the edge. Repeat on all the finger tips. Apply a thin layer of adhesive glue underneath the smile line edge of the nail. Attach the nail tip. Then, trim the nails to the desired length. Resin, gel, or acrylic can be applied to give the nail additional support.

Nail tip post-service

The nail tip post-service is conducted by making an appointment for the client. The following appointment may be needed in removal of the artificial tips, or in the conditioning of the nails and cuticles. The client may wish to purchase at home care products at this time. Some of the products that can be recommended are polishes, lotions, or top coats. In maintaining cleanliness and orderliness procedures, you can ensure that you will be ready for your next client. Glues should be securely closed to prevent drying out. Applicator tips may need to be cleaned with acetone. The used materials should be disposed of properly in the bag located on the side of the table. However, this bag should be discarded in a pail with a lid. The sanitization and disinfectant procedures should be followed at least 20 minutes prior to another customer's arrival.

Nail wrap application

In step 1, begin with the client's smallest finger on the left hand to remove the nail polish. Use a non-acetone remover for artificial nails. The cotton should be saturated while you count to ten, holding the solution to the nail. Stroke the cotton ball towards the free edge of the nail to remove the polish. Occasionally, you may need to use orangewood cotton tipped stick to remove all traces from the cuticle area. Repeat process on other hand. In step 2, lower the nails into the fingerbowl. The fingerbowl should be filled with warm, soapy water. Use a nail brush to gently clean the nails above the fingerbowl. Do not soak nails that will be requiring a nail wrap. In step 3, apply gentle pressure to cotton tipped orangewood stick in the process of pushing the cuticle back.

In step 4, sand or etch lightly over the nail using a fine abrasive. This etching will be useful in removing unwanted natural oils from the nail. These oils will reduce the adhesive qualities of your products. Nail wraps can be attached to natural nails or over artificial nail tips. However, in using an artificial nail tip, you will want to shape the free edges to fit the shape of the tip wells. In step 5, spray or treat the nail with an antiseptic for dehydrating the nail further. In step 6, use an adhesive to coat the surface of the nails. Allow the adhesive to dry. You may want to apply an activator to shorten the adhesives drying time. In step 7, the tip wells will need to be filed with a file or a tip blender.

In step 8, cut the fabric to form to the shape and size of the nail. Wipe your hands thoroughly to keep from contaminating the adhesive backed fabric as dust and debris could disrupt the adhesive process. In step 9, fabrics not having an adhesive backing, will require a droplet of adhesive to be applied to the midpoint of the nail. Do not apply adhesive to the cuticle area. This would cause lifting and separation of the product. In step 10, apply the fabric approximately 1/16 inches distanced from the cuticle. Use a thick piece of small sized plastic for the smoothing process. In step 11, Cut off all the edges neatly with a pair of tiny scissors. The fabric should be trimmed at a distance of 1/16 inches away from the sidewalls and free edge of the nail.

In step 12, a thin layer of adhesive is applied down the center of nail with an extender tip. Stay clear of the cuticle. The adhesive will soak into the fabric allowing the fabric to fasten itself. Use the plastic tool as you smooth out the fabric. In step 13, apply an adhesive dryer. Be careful not to touch the skin. In step 14, use extender tip to apply second layer of adhesive; ensuring that the free edge is sealed to eliminate product lifting. In step 15, another layer of adhesive dryer is required. In step 16, shape the nails with a medium fine abrasive. In step 17, Use block buffer on the nails after you have applied cuticle oil. Uneven areas of the fabric are smoothed out by the buffing. Be careful not to harm the wrap.

In step 18, have client wash nails with nail brush and soap at the sink facility. All dust, oil, and chemicals are to be removed from hands. In step 19, application of nail polish is completed. The post service includes the scheduling of another appointment, the client's opportunity to purchase polish, cuticle creams, lotions, top coats, polishes, or nail care implements. The nail technician should clean and organize her work space. Make sure caps are sealed on products. Oil used at the neck of the adhesive bottle will eliminate the cap sticking. Extender tips can be placed in a covered glass jar with acetone; using a toothpick to clean the end of the tip. Fabrics are stored in sealed containers. Used materials are disposed of properly. Sanitized and disinfect all tools at least 20 minutes prior to next service scheduled.

Maintenance

In step 1, the nail wrap pre-service is finished. In step 2, non-acetone polish removal is applied. In step 3, wash nails. In step 4, carefully, push back the cuticle. In step 5, smooth out the area of growth between the wrap and recent growth of nail with a nail file. In step 6, an application of antiseptic should be given. In step 7, Use a nail extender tip to apply a droplet of adhesive on the recent growth of the nail. In step 8, an application of adhesive dryer is administered. In step 9, an additional layer of adhesive is applied over the whole nail to fortify and seal the wrap. In step 10, another layer of adhesive dryer is applied. In step 11, shape nails with a medium/ fine abrasive. This ensures a smooth surface.

In step 12, buff the nails using a small drop of cuticle oil and block buffer. In step 13, use hand lotion and apply massage techniques to hands and arms. In step 14, use cotton to remove oil traces from nail. In step 15, application of nail polish should be accomplished. In step 16, complete all steps for post service procedures. In four week fabric wrap maintenance, step 1 through step 6 is the same. However in step 7, there is a need to cut more fabric for the nail wrap. This is done in an effort to resurface the recent growth and old nail wrap. Lay to the side until beginning step 9.

In step 8, adhesive is applied to the fill area and distributed over the recent growth area with an extender tip. Avoid contact with skin or cuticle. In step 9, application of the fabric resurfacing the recent growth on the nail. In step 10, an additional layer of adhesive is administered. In step 11, put on a layer of adhesive dryer to shorten the drying process. In step 12, put on more adhesive to cover the recent growth surface. In step 13, put on more adhesive dryer. In step 14, put on more adhesive resurfacing the entire nail in an effort to fortify and seal the new wrap with the old wrap. In step 15, put on more adhesive dryer. In step 16, shape the nail with a medium/ fine abrasive. This should create a smoother surface.

In step 17, use cuticle oil with the buffer block to create a high shine appearance. In step 18, use massage techniques and hand lotion to give a massage. In step 19, soak cotton in acetone and remove oil from nail. In step 20, application of nail polish is administered. In step 21, finish off with nail wrap post service procedures. Fabric wrap removals include nail wrap pre-service, soaking the nails, removing softened wraps, buffing nails, and conditioning the cuticles. Nails are soaked in a glass bowl with a one inch level of acetone solution. Use an orangewood stick or metal pusher to remove the old wraps. Use the fine buff blocker to remove leftover glue. Use cuticle oil and lotion for conditioning the skin and cuticle areas.

Paper wrap application

In step 1, the nail wrap pre-service includes adding a mending liquid, (a glue that dissolves polish remover), mending tissue, (light, delicate, tissue paper), and ridge filler to the work space. In step 2, the old nail polish is taken off. In step 3, the nails are scrubbed with soap and a nail brush. The client is instructed to finish washing hands at the sink facility. In step 4, the cuticles are pushed back gently with an orangewood stick or metal pusher. In step 5, nails are buffed until shine is removed with a medium/fine abrasive. In step 6, an application of nail antiseptic is administered. In step 7, the paper is applied in an effort to mend the nail. The paper has a feathered edge and can be tucked underneath the free edge of the nail.

In step 8, the paper tissue is soaked with the mending liquid. In step 9, use two fingers in positioning the wrap. In step 10, urged the tissue towards the free edge and the sidewalls with a metal pusher or orangewood stick. Place the pusher into the polish remover a few times over during this process. Keep working until the tissue has a smooth texture. In step 11, make sure that you leave enough to remaining tissue as you cut off any remaining tissue at a distance of 1/16 inch from the sidewalls. The remaining tissue will need to be tucked underneath the free edge of the nail. In step 12, put mending liquid on the underside of the free edge. In step 13, create a smooth texture on the free edge with the use of the pusher.

In step 14, buff nail and wrap lightly with a fine emery board to make the nail smoother. In step 15, put on two to three layers of mending liquid to cover the surfaces of the nail and the free edge. In step 16, put on ridge filler over the top surface of the nail. Ridge filler must be completely dry before additional applications of products are continued. In step 17, application of nail polish is administered to dry nails. Application of nail polish should begin with a base coat, followed by two color coats of polish. The final coat is a topcoat. Allow to dry. In step 18, finish off with nail wrap post service procedures. Post service includes scheduling of another appointment, client's opportunity to purchase products, organizing and sanitizing the workspace, equipment, and instruments.

Application of acrylic nails using forms

In step 1, nails receive a cleaning including removal of existing polish. In step 2, cuticle is pushed back with cotton tipped orangewood stick. In step 3, nails are buffed using medium/fine abrasive in an effort to remove existing natural oils from the nail. In step 4, antiseptic is applied to all the nails. In step 5, the nail forms come in different textures. The disposable nail form is positioned on the nail after paper backing has been removed. This placement requires the disposable nail to be formed to fit the client's nail shape. The form should be pressed on all surfaces to ensure adhesion. This includes the free edge of the nail. Reusable forms are positioned on the nail tight enough to allow a good fit, but not tight enough to cause discomfort.

In step 6, the technician and client wears safety equipment. This includes eye goggles, and the technician alone wears safety gloves. Only a minuscule droplet of primer should be applied to the natural nail. Do not use the nail brush to spread the primer. The primer will be distributed evenly across the surface of the nail if the nail is given time to rest. Do not apply heat or air to the hands to hurry the drying process. In step 7, use two containers: one containing liquid acrylic and the other containing powder acrylic. You may choose two color methods consisting of the following: one container of white tip powder, one container of clear, natural, or pink powder, and the last container of acrylic liquid. Clients are offered the opportunity to select color methods.

In step 8, lower brush into acrylic liquid, one way to make sure not to overload the brush with liquid is to wipe the brush along the edge of container before use. In step 9, the same brush is lowered into the acrylic powder and given a little bit of a spinning motion. A ball of acrylic product will be formed. The two color method requires use of white powder. In step 10, this ball is positioned at the beginning of the free edge delineation. In step 11, use the midline portion of the sable brush to adjust the acrylic to form the correct shape. Do not use painting strokes. Sidewall lines should be formed in a parallel shape. Also, natural free line of two color acrylic method ensures formation of the French manicures distinctive appearance.

In step 12, an additional ball of medium consistency acrylic is positioned on natural nail near the free edge line on the midpoint of the nail. In step 13, use same technique as before to shape the acrylic. In step 14, pink acrylic will form as small wet beads on the end of the brush. These beads require brushing over the entire surface of the nail. Keep the application thin to ensure a natural look. In step 15, continue with steps 5-14 for all the nails. In step 16, Take off the forms when the nails have thoroughly dry. A clicking sound when tapped is indicative of a dry nail. In step 17, shape nails with coarse/medium abrasive. Strokes should be applied in long, sweeping motions. Nails are shaped thin around cuticle, the free edge, and sidewalls.

In step 18, the nails are buffer until smooth with a block buffer. In step 19, application of cuticle oil is administered to cuticles, skin, and nails. In step 20, massage techniques and hand lotion are applied to hands and arms of the client. In step 21, the client uses soap and a nail brush to clean hands thoroughly. The client is instructed to rinse hands thoroughly in water and to dry completely. Hands should be dried with disposable towel. The client that has chosen the two color method requires application of a brush on sealer or a buffing to complete the service. In step 22, client's choosing one color acrylic nails are given a complete nail polishing service. This begins with a base coat, followed by two color coats of polish, with a topcoat.

Acrylic nails over tips or natural nails

In step 1, finish off the acrylic nail pre-service. In step 2, start with smallest finger on the left hand and remove nail polish. Work towards the thumb until all traces of nail polish have been removed. In step 3, have the client gently lower nails into the fingerbowl filled with warm, soapy water. Brush nails, rinse, and dry completely. In step 4, push back the cuticle with cotton tipped orangewood stick or a metallic pusher. In step 5, buff the nails with medium/ fine abrasives in order to remove the natural oils. Use a sanitized brush to remove dust and filing particles from the nail. In step 6, an application of nail antiseptic is administered. Nail antiseptic can be sprayed or applied with cotton. In step 7, nail tips are applied if previously requested.

In step 8, use plastic gloves for application of the primer. Both you and the client wear safety goggles during this step. A primer brush is used to apply a minuscule droplet of primer to natural nails. Allow time for the primer to distribute itself across the nail's surface. Do not try to paint the primer on the nail. Do not use heat or air to dry the nails prematurely. They should dry at room temperature. In step 9, use two small containers of acrylic liquid and powder. Use three bowls for white tip powder, pink powder, and acrylic liquid in the two color system. In step 10, lower the brush into the liquid, making sure to brush the sides of the container's lid to remove any brush that becomes overloaded with solution.

In step 11, lower the brush's end into the white acrylic powder for the two-color system. For the one color system, then lower the brush into clear or natural acrylics. Swirl gently and lift the brush out of the powder. Care should be shown when extracting for a larger or smaller nail size. The size of the acrylic ball extracted is in direct proportion to the nail size. In step 12, the ball of the acrylic is positioned on the free edge of the nail being serviced. In step 13, use the center part of the sable brush to press acrylic into desired shape on the nail. Sidewalls are formulated with parallel lines. Two color acrylic methods require shaping along natural free edge line with white powder in keeping with French manicure styles.

In step 14, an additional ball of acrylic consisting of a medium density is positioned on the nail bed along the free edge line in the middle of the nail. In step 15, the acrylic ball is pressed into a thin edge along the sidewalls and the cuticle. For two color methods, you will need to use the pink powder for this application. In step 16, the tip is cut or trimmed to the length desired. Ten, a tiny, moist bead of acrylic powder is dropped from the brush to the cuticle area. The brush's wetness will allow the bead to glide easily over the nail in this application. The acrylic should be maintained close to the cuticle, the sidewall, and free edge of the nail. This is in keeping with natural application procedures.

In step 17, coarse abrasives applied in shaping the free edge. Abrasive is reduced to medium then to finer applications as the nail is shaped. In step 18, nails are buffed creating a smooth nail exterior. In step 19, cuticle oil is applied to the skin and nail cuticles in a circular motion. In step 20, the nails are cleaned using the fingerbowl and a nail brush. Bails are rinsed, followed by drying with laundered or disposable towel. For two color methods, nails are given a brushed on sealer at this time and an additional buffing. In step 21, apply nail polish for the one color method using base coat, two coats of color, and a top coat nail polish. In step 23, finish the nail care service with the acrylic post-service methods.

Acrylic nail post-service procedures

The acrylic nail post-service procedures include scheduling another appointment. The acrylic nail upkeep requires a fill job administered every two to three weeks. Nails that grow rapidly will require earlier fills. Also, the client with acrylic nails will require a regular manicure sandwiched between the maintenance appointments. Clients should be given the opportunity to purchase products that will help in the home upkeep of the acrylic nails. Then, the table will need to be reset and sanitized for the next use. Disposable materials should be properly discarded. An acetone solution is used to clean the brush. Do not leave the brush in the acetone as the glue that holds the bristles in place will soften. Try avoiding the act of trimming the bristles. Do not pull them out either as both actions damage the brush. Keep the acrylic powders in a covered jar.

The final procedures include storage of primers and acrylic liquids in dark, low-temperatures. Products should never be kept near heat sources. Primer and acrylic liquids should not be kept if they have been moved to a container that is not the original container. Pour these solutions into a liquid absorbing paper towel. This should be secured in the plastic bag for disposal. Other materials requiring disposal include any materials or supplies that have been soiled with acrylic product. Then, secure the bag in the trash can with a lid. Rules and regulations must be strictly followed in the disposal process. The pre-service sanitation should be finished to completion at least 20 minutes prior to servicing of the next client. This includes sanitization of the table and all the implements. Reusable forms will also require sanitation for a period of 20 minutes.

Acrylic backfill with an electric file

In step 1, the nail polish is removed with an acetone based nail polish remover. In step 2, the cuticle is pushed back gently. In step 3, the new nail growth is prepared for refill treatment. In step 4, the nail is dusted. In step 5, a pencil is used to mark out the new smile line. This line is sketched at about 1/16 inch in front of the earlier smile line. In step 6, grasp the cylinder carbide bit at approximately 45 degrees, use medium pressure to score out a channel along the sketched line. In step 7, the score line is the guiding line to use in backfilling with a new application of white acrylic. In step 8, use acetone to dust off loose particles and to remove pencil lines.

In step 9, use brush to apply white acrylic ball to area just below the smile line. The flat side of the brush is used to move the acrylic towards the sidewalls. Acrylic is tapped lightly to flatten out white and pink areas in the nail bed. In step 10, once smile lines have all been backfilled, begin refill with pink acrylic. The final clear, acrylic ball will be applied in step 11. This is an optional treatment that seals the white and pink areas into one full surface. In step 12, the steps 17-21 are replicated for each nail surface. In step 13, nails may receive buffing with a three way buffer, top coat of high gloss top coat, acrylic sealant, or U.V. gel application. In step 14, post service procedure is provided.

Acrylic backfill without an electric file

In step 1, finish off the acrylic nail pre-service. In step 2, start with smallest finger on the left hand and remove nail polish. Work towards the thumb until all traces of nail polish have been removed. In step 3, have the client gently lower nails into the fingerbowl filled with warm, soapy water. Brush nails, rinse, and dry completely. In step 4, use a coarse file to level out the stress areas on both sides of the smile line. In step 5, a newly formed free edge will be created on the nail. Apply the white acrylic ball to the nail. In step 6, apply the pink acrylic product. The pink acrylic requires a placement above the smile line. Press ball to cover the stress area and sidewalls. In step 7, begin procedures following acrylic refill service.

Acrylic nail application on nail biters

In step 1; finish off the acrylic application pre-service. In step 2, removal of nail polish is accomplished beginning on the smallest finger and working towards the thumb. In step 3, nails are cleaned using a soapy water filled fingerbowl and brush. Nails are rinsed and dried. In step 4, push back of cuticle with a cotton tipped orangewood stick or a metal pusher is required. In step 5, buff nails with a medium/fine abrasive. Brush off loose particles when finished. In step 6, use cotton tipped orangewood stick or apply a spray of nail antiseptic. In step 7, apply primer to nail plate cautiously using plastic gloves. Both, you and the customer will wear protective, safety goggles. Do not touch skin and remember oversensitivity may be present due to nail biting habits.

In step 8, use separate jars for preparing the acrylic liquids and powders. In step 9, allow a tiny ball of acrylic to form in a medium density. This will be required for the two color method. In step 10, a tiny ball is applied directly to the skin in the proximity of the bitten nail. In step 11, the center of the brush is used to press the ball and shape the base. Be careful to keep the acrylic away from the sidewall line. In step 12, once the acrylic product has dried carefully separate the skin from the free edge line. This gives you a free edge that has the surface ability to support a nail form. In step 13, a nail form is placed on the free edge.

In step 14, position ball of medium density onto point where the nail form and the nail intersect. In step 15, the center of brush is applied to press and shape extension. The free edge should be formed to be a bit longer than the fingertips. This is done because a person that has a habit of nail biting is not accustomed to having lengthier nails. In step 16, an additional ball of acrylic is positioned near the free edge line in the middle of the nail. For two color methods, you will use pink powder. In step 17, press acrylic towards sidewalls and cuticles thinly on the surface. In step 18, apply tiny, moist beads to cuticle region. For two color methods, you will continue to use the pink powder.

In step 19, nail forms are placed over dry nail surfaces. You can tell that the nails are dry enough for the nail forms when the nails make a hard, tapping sound. In step 20, shape and form the free edge with a coarse/medium abrasive. In step 21, nails are buffed. In step 22, cuticle oil is massaged into skin and nails. In step 23, hand cream is applied. This if followed by a massage of the arms and hands. In step 24, nails are washed using warm, soapy water in fingerbowl and a brush. Rinse hands, and then dry with disposable towel. For two color methods, an application of brush on sealers or buffing is administered at this point. In step 25; finish off with the acrylic application post-service procedures.

Acrylic nail refills

In step 1; finish off the acrylic application pre-service. In step 2, follow procedures for removal of nail polish. In step 3, a medium/fine abrasive is used to level out the uneven area found between the recent growth surfaces and the nail plate. In step 4, use the flat side of the abrasive to shape the nail, keeping the free edge thin. In step 5, the nails are buffed. In step 6, check and repair lifting of product with a file. In step 7, the nails are washed, but not soaked. In step 8, cuticles are pushed back. In step 9, nails are buffed with a medium/fine abrasive. Remove loose particles with a brush. In step 10, nail antiseptic is administered to nail surface. You will use orangewood stick, spray, or cotton ball for this antiseptic application.

In step 11, the nail primer is applied using safety equipment for yourself and your client. Do not use the brush that comes with the primer. Instead, apply minuscule amount of primer with primer brush. Then, allow primer to spread out on its own covering nail region. Air or heat should not be applied to speed up drying time. The primer is dry when it turns to a chalky white color. In step 12, acrylic liquid and powders are readied for application. In step 13, apply balls of acrylic to the recent growth of nail. For two color methods, use the pink acrylic product. In step 14, center of brush is applied in pressing motion to shape product over nail. In step 15, tiny, moist balls of product are positioned at base of the nail nearest cuticle.

In step 16, wetness of the brush is useful for sliding the beads over nail. Acrylic goes along the cuticle, sidewall, and free edge of the nails when finished. For two color methods, the pink powder acrylic is used. In step 17, nails are checked for dryness. The nails will make a sharp tapping sound when they are dried. Then, use coarse/medium abrasives for filing and shaping the free edge. This is reduced to medium/fine abrasive as shape is perfected. The nail should be formed in a thin, tapered shape towards the cuticle, nail tip, and sidewalls. If the customer has a recent growth of 4-5 weeks, then your customer may desire to switch from the two color method to the one color method. One color methods: Files back the white free edge or backfill the nail.

In step 18, the nail is buffed. You will use a block buffer for this step. In step 19, you will apply cuticle oil to the skin, cuticle regions, and nails. Cuticle oil is administered to these surfaces with the use of an orangewood stick wrapped in cotton. In step 20, hand cream is applied. This is followed by massage techniques administered to the hands and arms. This can increase the pleasure and relaxation of the client making your services highly desired. In step 20, the nails are cleaned with the use of warm, soapy water in the fingerbowl and a brush. Rinse and dry with a disposable towel. In step 22, apply a base coat, two color coats, and a top coat of nail polish. In step 23; finish off using the acrylic application post service.

Acrylic nail crack repair procedures

In step 1; finish off acrylic application pre-service. In step 2, remove old nail polish from nail surfaces. In step 3, use file to form a "V" into the crack of the acrylic. You may also choose to file this surface flat in an effort to smooth out the crack. In step 4, nails are washed, rinsed, and dried. In step 5, administer the application of nail antiseptics to the surfaces of the nails. In step 6, use safety equipment for yourself and your client in the application of the nail primer. Remember to use only a minuscule amount of primer as a little goes a long way. In step 7, nail form may be needed to give large cracked surfaces additional support. In step 8, ready the acrylic liquid and powders in their own separate containers.

In step 9, apply beads of product on cracked regions. For two color system, use color indicated. In step 10, nails are shaped as acrylic is pressed into cracks. In step 11, use acrylic balls to fill out cracked surfaces. Shape nail. More acrylic may be required depending upon damage. If more products are required, then shape and allow drying times. In step 12, form used will be taken off. In step 13, nail is reshaped into desired form. In step 14, nails are buffed. In step 15, wash, rinse, and dry nails. In step 16, cuticle oil is applied to skin, cuticle, and nail regions. In step 17, rub hands and arms. In step 18, wash, rinse, and dry nails. In step 19, nail polish. In step 20; finish off using acrylic application post service procedures.

Acrylic removal

In step 1, put enough acetone in a glass bowl to cover the client's fingertips with the solution. In step 2, set the client's fingertips in the solution for 15 minutes to loosen the acrylic from the nails. The acrylic removal product should be used in accordance with the manufacturer's recommendations. In step 3, you will use a metal pusher or orangewood stick to remove the loosened acrylic product from the nail. It is highly recommended that you do not use nippers or nail cutters to remove the loosened product as this may cause excessive harm to the nail plate surface. In step 4, nails are buffed using a fine block buffer. This will remove any acrylic particles remaining on the nail. In step 5, the skin and cuticle regions require the application of cuticle lotions and hand lotion conditioners.

Light cured gel application procedures

In step 1, start on smallest finger of left hand in removal of nail polish. In step 2, wash, rinse, and dry nails. In step 3, administer a nail antiseptic to the nail surfaces. In step 4, push back the cuticles carefully with the use of a metal pusher or orangewood stick wrapped in cotton. In step 5, buff nails with medium/fine abrasive. Use a brush on remaining loose particles. In step 6, client may choose nail tips at this juncture. Apply tips, followed by cutting and shaping. Then, apply a coat of gel to surface and edge of tip in an effort to seal and protect it from damage. This seal must remain intact throughout the rest of the manicure. White tips with cut out smile lines should be used when applying French manicure.

In step 7, nails should be prepared in accordance with manufacturer's directions; usually gels don't need a primer, instead the use of a base coat gel or bonder is used. In step 8, the first gel is applied over the surface, and the surface edges. This gel is the base coat gel. Remove excessive gel touching cuticles with orangewood stick. Discard stick. In step 9, use lamp to cure the gel following the time guidelines from the product manufacturer. In step 10, apply steps 8-9 on right hand. Then, apply to thumbs of right and left hand. In step 11, use second gel on the left hand. This gel is the building gel. It is positioned generously from the middle of the cuticle to the free edge surface. Just apply gel to the fingers, not the thumbs.

In step 12, position the hand under the lamp for a period of 20 seconds to cure. The lamp "freezes" the gel to the point that more applications of thinner products can be applied. In step 13, continue steps 11-13 on right hand. In step 14, continue in performing same steps on the thumbs. In step 15, a smaller portion of gel is distributed down one side of the gel line. Then the stroke is repeated until the gel is wrapped across the nail and seals the free edge of the four fingers. This creates a protective sealant around the free edge of nail. In step 16, allow hand to cure under lamp. In steps

17, steps 15 and 16 continue on right hand. In step 18, continue in performing the same steps on the thumbs.

In step 19, use a cleaner in accordance with the manufacturer's instructions in removing sticky particles from nail surfaces. Normally, these cleaners will have an acetone or alcohol base. In step 20, a 180 grit abrasive is recommended in filing the contours of the gel nails. The sidewalls and free edge require a gentle, down stroke with the bevel. Remember to grasp the bevel at a 45 degree angle from the top middle dome towards the free edge. In step 21, nails are buffed. Use a nylon manicure brush in removing loose particles. In step 22, use polish stokes in the application of a small portion of gel over the nails. Wrap the free edge in gel sealant. In step 23, continue steps 16-19 on other hand. In step 24, rub hand cream into arms and hands. In step 25, wash, rinse, and dry nails. In step 26, apply base coat, two color coats, and top coat to nails, if desired. Gel application procedures are completed at the end of the light cured gel.

Concluding an apointment

In step 1, make another appointment for your client. In step 2, recommend products for client's use to maintain her treatment at home. Recommended products are polish lotion, top coats, and hand lotions. In step 3, clean and organize the table for reuse. The table should be set up for use by the next client. Check that supplies are restocked. In step 4, dispose of materials using proper procedures. In step 5, pre-service sanitization methods are applied. Implements require sanitization for 20 minutes or state recommended timeframes before reuse.

Light-cured gel over forms

In step 1, stock the light-cured gel supplies, and nail forms in an organized fashion on the manicure table. In step 2, position the nail forms on the fingers and thumbs. Do not use nail forms that have not been sanitized for use. In step 3, administer a small amount of gel on the natural nail. The nail form should not receive an application of gel at this time. In step 4, allow the gel to cure before going on to step 5. In step 5, shape the gel around the free edge of the nail. In step 6, allow the gel to cure. In step 7, cover the nail, the nail form's surface, and the free edge with gel. In step 8, allow the gel to cure. In step 9, discard nail forms or remove non-disposable ones for later sanitization.

In step 10, form free edge on nail. In step 11, additional application of gel is given to the surface of nail. In step 12, allow gel to cure. In step 13, use an acetone or alcohol based cleaner on the nail to remove sticky substances. In step 14, recommended use of 180 grit abrasive will create good curvatures on the gel nail. Remember to grasp the bevel at a 45 degree angle with a downward stroke that moves from the center of the nail to the free edge. In step 15, nails are buffed. Use of a nylon manicure brush is recommended in lifting off debris. In step 16, a top coat gel is administered. Careful, downward strokes are applied. The gel is applied to the surfaces and the free edge of the nail's tip.

In step 17, steps 12-13 are continued on other hand. In step 18, small measure of cuticle oil is massaged into skin and nails. In step 19, rub hand lotion into hands and nails using massage techniques. In step 21, base coat, two color coats, and top coat is applied. In step 22; finish off with a gel application post-service. In step 1, of the gel application post service, make another appointment for your client. In step 2, recommend products for client's use to maintain her treatment at home. In step 3, clean and organize the table for reuse. Check and restock all supplies. In step 4, dispose of materials. In step 5, pre-service sanitization methods are applied. Implements require sanitization for 20 minutes or state recommended timeframes before reuse.

No-light gel application procedures

In step 1; finish off the acrylic application pre-service. In step 2, removal of nail polish is accomplished beginning on the smallest finger and working towards the thumb. In step 3, nails are cleaned using a soapy water filled fingerbowl and brush. Nails are rinsed and dried. In step 4, push back of cuticle with a cotton tipped orangewood stick or a metal pusher is required. In step 5, buff nails with a medium/fine abrasive. Brush off loose particles when finished. In step 6, use cotton tipped orangewood stick or apply a spray of nail antiseptic. In step 7, apply nail tips if decided on during client consultation. In step 8, use a brush to apply a thin coat of gel to all five nails of the left hand. Avoid touching the cuticle with the gel solution.

In step 9, for activator-cured gels: spray approximately 8 inches away from nail. This reduces problems associated with heat reactions. For water cured gels: submerge nails in water according to manufacturer's instructions. Time limits are usually for periods of about 2-5 minutes. In step 10, continue procedures on other hand. In step 11, second coating of gel is applied if needed. Not all gels require second coatings. In step 12, use medium fine abrasive to form nails. In step 13, nails are buffed. In step 14, cuticle oil is applied. In step 15, rub hand lotion into hands and arms using massage techniques. In step 16, wash, rinse, and dry nails. In step 17, apply a base coat, two color coats, and a top coat to nails. In step 18; finish off with a gel application post service.

Gels and allergens

The product applied erroneously typically can be traced back to the incorrect hardening of the gel. The product may have been applied too rapidly. The product may have not had enough drying time under the light. The lamp unit may have had a dirty bulb or an old bulb which altered the effectiveness of the U.V. bulb. Filings may produce allergens and dust which can enhance exposure. Beads should be of a medium, dry consistency and should form a smooth band when placed on the natural tip or nail. If the solution is runny, then it is not the right consistency. Smaller brushes should be used to give more control. Special blends have been known to cause chemical imbalances in the product. Thirty percent of all nail technicians will experience a skin problem. Work related allergens can be avoided when safety precautions are strictly followed.

Combining no-light gels and fiberglass or silk wrap applications

In step 1, cut strips or use pre-cut fiberglass. Strips range from ¼ inch wide and ½ inch long strips. Lengths will need to be trimmed to the size of nail. In step 2, fiberglass or silk strip is positioned in a diagonal direction across wet surface. A second strip is placed forming an "x" across the nail. In step 3, apply more gel. Follow with activation for gels. There are two types: activator-cured gels: spray approximately 8 inches away from nail. For water cured gels: submerge nails in water according to manufacturer. Use medium fine abrasive to form nails. Buff nails, and apply cuticle oil. Rub hand lotion and massage. Then, wash, rinse, and dry nails. Apply base coat, two color coats, and top coat to nails. Finish off with gel application post service.

Nail art

Nail art has a few basic guidelines to follow. It is suggested that you approach nail art with an open mind. This is an art form that may require some patience and practiced techniques. However, it is expected that you will be able to master this form given the right opportunities for practice. Exposure to various techniques is recommended. Pay attention to your client's wishes, lifestyle, and comfort zones before advising the client to obtain this service. This form of art must be practiced, but it is not unattainable. However, it is recommended that you give yourself ample time to perform the service once scheduled. Display your perfected art designs in an attractive manner.

Price your services at a reasonable amount making sure to count time involved, cost of materials, and experience levels. Purchase quality tools, including a pair of stork shears used in nail art.

Free hand painting and flat nail art

Flat nail art requires the use of the following brushes: round brush, liner brush, flat brush, bright brush, fan brush, spotter brush, striper brush, and others used in specialized techniques. The round brush has a narrowed end with a large belly. This brush will hold a large amount of paint and water. Also, this brush is useful due to its flexibility and use in blocking techniques. The narrowed end of this brush gives it versatility. The liner brush is useful in creating details found in linework, outlining, and lettering. The flat brush is useful as a shading brush. The square end and long bristles can be used for flat, long strokes. It can also give a chiseled edge with a fine line. This brush should be used when you have a need to double load, blend, or shade.

Animal designs and leaves

Some designs include animal stripes. Tiger stripes are created from gold, bronze, copper, and black nail paints or polishes. Other vibrant colors may also be selected. With the liner brush, load the lower three quarters of the brush. Stop midpoint along the nail. Pull brush across creating a wavy pattern. Make sure you lift it up and away as you pull towards the stop point. Continue until you have created a pattern down one side allowing for the additional colors to be filled in after drying of initial pattern.

Width and dimension are exhibited in shading techniques with two shades of green. Begin with the flat brush and pivot one quarter turn to the left or right. Follow through with a lift, pulling up towards the end of the stroke to create a leaf.

Brushes and heart designs

The bright brush has a stiff, short, flat brush. The fan brush has similar structures useful for blending, and special effects. The spotter brush is short, with a small tip used for detailing. The striper has an assortment of sizes and is used on long lines, striping effects, or animal prints. The marbelizer is a stylus which has an assortment of sizes useful in creating polka dots, eyes, bubbles, marbleized textures, and a variety of other effects.

The heart design is created with three dots on a painted inverted triangle shape. The detailer is used to connect the dots, on its center make a "v" shape. Round the edge from the top until you reach the lower dot. At this point, you will join all the dots in a "v" formation to form a heart.

Flower petals

Flower petals are created with a loaded #2 flat brush. Double load the brush with a darker color and a lighter color on each side of the bristle. The tip of the brush is positioned flat on the nail about halfway up. Then, pivot the side of the brush in a one quarter turn, lightening up on the touch as you pivot. Pull the brush towards the end of the petal and lift up towards the end of the stroke, creating a teardrop or leaf shape. Do not position the darker color over the lighter color as you make work on your highlights. In creating a petal with a 10/0 liners use the tip of the brush and pull the brush to make a "C" shape or comma stroke. Taper the stroke towards this end of this method.

Gold leaf application

In step 1, allow polish nails to completely dry. In step 2, use an adhesive on the region of the nail that is to be covered in the foil. In step 3, position the bits of foil on the nail with the use of tweezers or a fresh orangewood stick. Carefully press the foil down into the wet adhesive. In step 5, if gems or striping tape is desired, then apply those items at this time. You can move on to the application of the sealer only when the surface has completely dried. Apply a clear coat of nail polish. In step 6, once this layer has dried, you can begin the application of a second layer of clear polish. Allow that layer to dry slightly, before the application of the third layer of clear nail polish.

Airbrushing

In step 1, the client pays for services before application of the airbrush nail service. At this time the client makes departure preparations. In step 2, the client is instructed to use the nail brush in an effort to remove dust or oil particles from the nail surfaces. The client washes, rinses, and dries nail thoroughly. Inspect upon completion as water and oil could prevent a professional application. In step 3, the nails receive a base coat over the nail plate surface and the free edge. In step 4, enclose your hand over the clients. The overspray will fall on your hand and not your client. Your thumb will be in position slightly up over the cuticle region. This paint will wash off with sanitization procedures. In step 5, coax the paint down the nail without touching the bristles to the nail surface.

In continuing with step 5, bonder is used on the polish brush to prevent any scratches or drags. This should cover all the sides and free edges. In step 6, do not touch the skin as it is extremely hard to remove. Finally, apply top coat or sealer with 2-3 minute drying time. In step 7, cover entire nail with protective glaze. Then, allow drying for about 10 minutes. In step 8, cleanse nails using the procedures provided by the manufacturer of product. Nails can be lightly dried, but do not smudge painted surfaces. Excessive overspray is removed with application of alcohol or cuticle oil. In step 9, quick dry product is applied and allowed to dry for 30 minutes. In step 10, check results. In step 11, use an acetone based nail polish remover, if necessary.

Two color fade

In step 1, use a base coat of crystalline, special effect, or white to hide dark tones or in the application of transparent nail paints. In step 2, use the start up procedure provided by the product manufacturer to ensure proper application methods. Load your gun with pain. Then, check that it sprays evenly. Finally, apply a dry, coat with moving in a diagonal pattern over the top two thirds of the nail. Your arm should move with the motion. You may choose to do more than one nail. For a lighter, softer look put on fewer coats nearest the center of the nail. Nearest the cuticle area, you will want more coats of paint. In step 3, the right consistency of paint is applied nearest the cuticle region blending softly towards the center of the nail.

In step 4, the airbrush is changed to another color of choice. The second color is applied from the bottom up two thirds of the nail. A transition color will form when the two colors overlap. In step 5, a dry even coat of spray is given to the nail. Move in a diagonal pattern over the bottom two thirds of the nail. Your arm should move with the motion. You may choose to do more than one nail. For a lighter, softer look put on fewer coats nearest the center of the nail. In step 6, a top coat is applied to seal the nails and to give them added strength. This is an appropriate time to inform the client of the proper procedures for home maintenance. Remember to thoroughly clean your airbrush and all tips.

French manicure

In step 1, use a French or crystalline base coat of a neutral color for the nail tip. If you desire, you may skip airbrushing the base coat and go on to step 4. In step 2, the French manicure color is applied with a light misting spray. This spray can be transparent or opaque colored. If you desire, you may add a drop or two of distilled water to create a more transparent effect. In step 3, an optional coating of gold highlights or shimmer is applied over the French beige color. In step 4, the following steps are given in the use of a stencil: use a store bought stencil or curved paper positioned in very close proximity to the nail; the nail tip is left exposed for application of paint.

In continuing with step 4, self adhesive masks are an alternative. A white application of paint is applied. Pay attention to any run-offs or drips. Do not move stencil from nail to clean or dry it. Use blown air for drying. Add more applications of color until desired color has been obtained. In step 5, roll fingernail in slanted direction to line up the rounded edge of the nail with the white tip. In step 6, a lunula or moon is created with the stencil. The lunula receives a lighter application of nail tip color. In step 7, an application of nail bonder is applied and allowed to sit for 3 minutes for drying purposes. In step 8, French manicure is advised for the toenails. In step 9, toes are bonded, glazed, and cleansed with an airbrush paint cleanser.

Aromatherapy

Aromatherapy was a term first used by a French chemist named Rene' Maurice Gattefosse' in the year of 1928. It has been suggested in various research studies that aromatherapy can influence moods through the nasal passages which are connected to the emotion and memory portions of the brain. Down through the centuries; Ancient Egyptians, Chinese, Indians, and other cultures were aware of the effects of aromatic herbs and oils in their beauty and health treatments. Essential oils are extracted for use. Extraction methods are varied. Essential oils can be useful in the preparation of manicure, pedicure, massage, reflexology, and facial treatments. Some of the list of oils include: Lavender, Chamomile, Marjoram, Rosemary, Tea Tree, Cypress, Peppermint, Eucalyptus, Bergamot, and Geranium. Some carrier oils or base oils are Sweet Almond Oil, Apricot Oil, Avocado Oil, Grape seed Oil, and Jojoba Oil.

<u>Age deterrent</u>

In creating an age deterrent: blend 15 drops Lemon, 10 drops Lime, 5 drops Rosemary, 5 drops Lavender, 1 drop Spearmint, and 1 ounce of Grape Seed Oil. Use 2-3 drops of solution on age spots. Do not use the oil on the nails as the Lemon and Lime may cause damage to the nails. Massage hand 3-4 times. After about the third application, you should see a noticeable fading of the discoloration.

<u>Decadent manicure</u>

In creating decadent manicures, have candles with aromatic qualities lit. Use heavy cream and essential oils as a soaking solution. Lavender is a good selection for clients who are feeling stressed. Peppermint may be used for clients who need revitalization. Vanilla is a comforting smell and perfect for use in the winter months. In addition, play some calming music in the background to create a more relaxing mood for the client.

<u>Nail strengthening treatment</u>

In creating a nail strengthening treatment, blend together 20 drops of lemon, 15 drops of carrot oil, 13 drops of Grape Seed, 13 drops of Rosemary, 13 drops of Avocado Oil, and 2 ounces of Jojoba oil. Use a dark colored bottle for storage of ingredients. These ingredients are light sensitive and will do much better stored in a dark environment. This solution is useful when applied near the cuticle after the nails have been polished. Some clients will prefer a natural nail care treatment and will appreciate the use of this natural mix.

Cuticle softener

In creating a cuticle softener, blend together, 15 drops of carrot oil, 12 drops peppermint, 12 drops Eucalyptus, and 2 ounces of Jojoba oil. Store this solution in similar fashion to the nail strengthening treatment. Rub the oil into the cuticle as a conditioner.

Decadent pedicure

Use 1-2 cups of heavy cream mixed into 25 drops of your favored essential oil or 3 fragrant salt crystals. Candles and spa music add to the mood. Allow the client a 5-10 minute soak in the solution before performing the pedicure.

Therapeutic blends

Calming oils include: Lavender, Vetiver, Rosemary, Sandalwood, Ylang Ylang. Ambient Oils include: Vanilla, Cinnamon, Orange, Pine, Jasmine, Lavender, Bayberry, Rose, cherry, Lemon. Invigorating Oils include: Eucalyptus, Peppermint, Spearmint, Lemon, Orange, Geranium, jasmine, and Fennel. Oils that clear the minds: Rosemary and Cypress. Romantic Oils include: Ylang Ylang, Jasmine, and Sandalwood. Oils that are good for Foot Odors include: Sage and Baking Powder. Bactericide: Cinnamon, Clove, Lemon, Eucalyptus, Lavender, Pine, Grapefruit, and Lime. Abrasions: Tea Tree, Lavender, and Eucalyptus. Barber's Rash: Lemongrass, Geranium, and Peppermint. Nail Infections: Tea Tree. Oily Skin: Bergamot, Geranium, Clary Sage, Pettigraine and Cedar wood.

Dry, cracked heels

In creating a recipe for dry, cracked heels use 10 drops Rose, 5 drops Chamomile, 5 drops Geranium, and 5 drops of Pettigraine. Use 8-10 drops of this natural solution in a massage prior to the pedicure. At pedicure's final moments, add 3-4 drops on each heel using a massaging technique. This may require a few applications before the desired softness and suppleness is returned to the skin.

Swollen feet

In creating a recipe for swollen feet, use 15 drops Lavender, 15 drops Chamomile, 15 drops Rosemary, 15 drops Fennel, and 4 ounces of Jojoba Oil. Massage 25-30 drops of this natural solution into skin to improve the blood flow. Put feet up after the massage at an elevation above the person's heart. The client's feet should rest in this position for a period of about 10-15 minutes.

Fingernail shapes

The square nail has no curvature on the nail tip; the length is determined by the client. The squoval nail is best used for clients who use their hands frequently. This nail shape has a stronger full width near the free edge of the nail. The free edge has been rounded off and the tip of the nail extends just past the finger tip. The pointed nail is tapered with a longer nail. This nail can add a look of slenderness to the hand. The round nail is the preferred nail of male clients as it is somewhat pointed in appearance and is shaped to extend to just beyond the tip of the finger. The square nail has no curved edges and is cut straight and square at the end of the nail. The square nail can be alternate lengths.

Selection of shape

Shape of the hands, length of fingers, shape of the cuticles, and the daily use of the hands should be a consideration during the client consultation. The client consultation will enlist these factors to assist the client in making an informed selection. There is some attention given by some technicians to the shape of the cuticles as a mirror to how the fingernails should be shaped. In general the five shapes of the hand are the square nail, the squoval nail, the round nail, the oval nail, and the pointed nail. The selection of a long nail may not be the most appropriate for a person that uses their hands on the keyboard, assembly line, gardening, or sports. Additionally, many male clients tend to prefer a natural shape. Most professionals who display their hands will select a longer nail shape.

Important terms

Bevel: file down the uneven free edge of the nail with an emery board to make it smooth.

Chamois buffer: chamois cloth utilized to make the nail shine and to give the nails an even appearance.

Effleurage: a low key circular movement massage that relaxes and soothes.

Lacquer: a colored polish which contains nitrocellulose or amyl acetate. Chemicals evaporate rapidly. Some colored polishes contain castor oil which slows the drying process.

Mild abrasives: tin oxide, talc, silica, or kaolin utilized as a sanding agent in dry nail polish.

Oval nail: a square nail with somewhat curved corners used by professionals.

Styptic powder: powdered alum utilized to stop minor bleeding that can happen at the time of a manicure.

Petrissage kneading movement: massage used to boost blood flow with kneading movements in opposite directions.

Pledgets: small pieces of moistened cotton balls used to remove nail polish.

Pointed nail: a tapered, lengthier nail used to add a trim look to the hand.

Pumice powder: dry nail polish utilized along with the chamois buffer to enhance the nail's shiny appearance.

Round nail: the preferred nail of male clients that is somewhat pointed in appearance to the nail that just beyond the tip of the finger.

Square nail: no curved edges with a straight square cut at the end of the nail. The nail can be alternate lengths.

Squoval nail: most popular in clients who work extensively with their hands. This nail has a stronger full width near the free edge of the nail. The free edge has been rounded off and the tip of the nail extends just past the finger tip.

Massages: rubbing, pinching, kneading, and rhythmic rub down of the body that has restorative results.

Massage oils: mixture of oils relating to the lubrication, motorization, and rejuvenation of the skin in the course of a massage or a pedicure.

Nail rasp: angled edge, metallic file used to file in one direction.

Pedicure: cutting, shaping, polishing, massaging of toenails and feet.

Petrissage: rub down in a kneading motion that involves lifting, squeezing, and compression of the fleshy tissue.

Scrubs: mild, abrasives that softens calluses, or dry skin from the feet.

Soaks: commodities used to create a soft texture on the skin of the feet. The commodities used during the pedicure bath should include mild soaps, moisturizers, softening agents, deep infiltrating, and surface active elements.

Tapotement: beating technique used in massages or rub downs.

Curette: an implement that resembles a spoon used to clean debris out from the edge of the nail.

Cuticle nippers: an implement used to cut away dead skin from around the nail bed.

Diamond nail file: an implement made from metal and diamond dust. The sanitization of this file is fairly easy as it can readily be placed in disinfectant solutions.

Effleurage: an easy, consistent stroking rub down that is applied with the fingers and palms.

Foot files or paddles: a paddle sized sanding file that is used to smooth the callus and dry skin off of the foot.

Friction movement: a side to side foot compression applied with a firm force with the thumb to the bottom of the foot.

Hand manipulation: procedures used in massaging and treatment of the hands.

Toenail nippers: a curved or straight cutting appliance used to trim the toenails.

Pedicure station: a client's chair with armrests, a footrest, the nail technician's chair, or there are furniture pieces that are designed with all of these elements.

Pedicure stool: the low stool with or without a foot rest used by the nail technician.

Pedicure bath: this tub is also referred to as the basin and is useful for submersion of both of the client's feet.

Toe separators: foam pads used to keep the toes separated or from touching in the pedicure.

Calluses: rough growths on the skin.

Antifungal foot spray: a mild antiseptic combined with an antifungal mist used to treat the foot.

Pedicure slippers: disposable or foam slippers worn by clients who have worn closed toe shoes.

Bit: refers to burrs or part used to file the nail.

Concentric: the bits are balanced to perform in a balanced spin inside the motor.

Flutes: carbide bits are measured to reflect the amount of cuts in each bit. For instance, the larger flutes have coarse carbide bits. The smaller flutes have finer carbide bits.

Grit: the smaller the number, the more coarse the grit or sanding ability.

Revolutions per minute (RPMs): the number of times the bit revolves or spins in a given minute.

Rings of fire: this refers to the painful situation of having the barrel's flat edge of the electric file dig into the natural nail bed near the cuticle.

Torque: the measured amount per square inch or horsepower that describes the resistance in the electric file as the bit turns around.

Acrylic: a substance used to give strength to the nail tips.

Abrasive: any physical, coarse surface that has qualities which tend to sand or take the shine off of another surface.

Buffer block: a small, rectangular shaped block that is used to smooth or shine the nails.

Nail adhesive: a glue or sticky substance that bonds the nail tip to the natural nail.

Nail tip: a plastic, nylon, or acetate artificial nail that is used on the end of a natural nail. This artificial tip is used to create an extension in the length of the natural nail.

Tip cutter: a rounded, instrument used to cut off the tip of the nail.

Tip well cutting: recent, technique that is used to create smile lines. The smile lines will have white tips or traditional tips.

Silk: tight woven fabric that turns translucent when adhesive is spread over the material.

Stress strip: 1/8 inch piece of fabric used to mend or strengthen a split in the nail.

Acrylic nails: enhancements for the nail that are made by mixing acrylic liquids and powders.

Backfill: every 4-6 weeks the nails require trimming of the free edge and the replacement of the smile line.

Catalyst: the chemical helper that causes the explosion that creates heat.

Cyanoacrylate: rapid, setting sticky glue. It typically, is used with brush on or dip in acrylic powders.

Fills: when acrylic has been applied to newly grown nail. The nail typically needs fills applied every two to three weeks.

Odorless acrylics: acrylic substances without odor or evaporative qualities. This tendency gives the nail technician more time to work before drying occurs.

Fabric wraps: silk, linen, or fiberglass coverings.

Fiberglass: a strong, lasting, yet, thin synthetic mesh that has a weave in the fabric. This gives the glue or adhesive access.

Linen: a closely woven, weighty fabric that has an opaque quality. This remains constant even after the adhesive is applied. Only colored polishes will hide the opaque color.

Liquid nail wrap: polish consisting of tiny fibers used to fortify and safeguard natural nail growth.

Nail wraps: cloth or paper layers that fit the nail and are fastened to the top of the nail plate with nail adhesive or glue.

Paper wraps: paper, temporary nail coverings. These coverings will break up easily with the application of an acetone or a non-acetone remover.

Repair patch: section of fabric used to cover breaks or cracks in a damaged nail.

Photo initiators: attributes found in light cured acrylics harden after exposure to U.V. or ultraviolet rays.

Polymer: monomers join to form lengthy chains.

Polymerization: the transfer of heat from one polymer bead to another.

Reaction: when a liquid monomer is changed into a polymer.

Rebalancing: outline of the nail is filled to keep the natural look of the nail.

Activator-cured: technique uses a gel activator application to cure or set the product.

Halogen bulb: source of light used to cause the nail gel to harden.

Light-cured gel: gel variety hardens under an ultraviolet or halogen bulb.

No-light gel: gel variety requires water activation or sprayed on gel activators to harden.

Ultraviolet bulb: bulb gives off rays that are invisible to the naked eye.

Water-cured: water immersion technique used to harden no-light gels.

Free hand painting: one of most costly ways of design with a brush and skill. The other name for this technique is flat nail art.

Gems: jewelry used to add a decorative element to nail art.

Gravity-fed: when paint is drawn through the airbrush system by a force of gravity.

Internal mix: mixture of airbrush paint with air stored in airbrush.

Leafing: foil of gold, silver, or other colors used to create the nail art.

Mask knife: knife that has one cutting side. Used for cutting designs from mask paper or plastic materials.

Mask paper: paper used for creating designs.

Nail art: creative treatment gives customized service to clients.

Needle: part of the fluid nozzle on airbrush that allows only a measured portion of paint to be discharged at any given time.

Air hose: a tube that provides the connection between the airbrush compressor and the airbrush.

Color fade: a faint, subtle coloring technique that is used to blend colors across the nail simultaneously.

Color wheel: a tool used to select the primary, secondary, tertiary, or complementary colors.

Complementary colors: these colors are found on the color wheel on opposing sides.

Floating the bead: the brush floats across the application of a minuscule droplet on the nail.

Fluid nozzle: the tip of the nozzle that permits the needle of the airbrush to discharges paint onto a surface.

Foiling: a foil adhesive is used to make color patterns on the nail.

French Manicure: a natural appearance created with a white tip on the free edge of the nail.

Position: the word that refers to the straight up and down or laid down grasp used to hold brush in place.

Pressure: compression applied in stoking or painting motion when applying nail art paint.

Pull: paint flows from brush in uniformed manner.

Primary colors: colors not formed from a mixture of colored pigments.

Secondary colors: colors that can be mixed from combining two primary colors. These colors are directly across from the primary colors on color wheel.

Stencil: decorative tools used of pre-cut plastic, papers, or fabrics.

Striping tape: sticky tape placed over polished nails to create a design using a variety of colored tapes.

Tertiary colors: mixture of one part primary to one part of its closest color found on color wheel.

Well: reservoir or cup located at top of the brush for storage of excess paint.

Nail Technician Practice Test

1. Where should clean metal implements used for nail care be stored?
    a. In a jar with sanitizing liquid
    b. On a towel
    c. In a special case
    d. On a metal tabletop

2. Horizontal lines on the nail plate are known as
    a. hyponychium.
    b. leukonychia.
    c. Beau's lines.
    d. koilynychia.

3. What is the highest temperature at which flammable nail products should be stored?
    a. 80°F
    b. 100°F
    c. 120°F
    d. 140°F

4. What is the purpose of a paraffin treatment for the hands?
    a. To clean the cuticles
    b. To improve the absorption of lotion
    c. To remove nail polish
    d. To strengthen the nail

5. What should a technician do if blood is drawn during a manicure?
    a. Send the client home
    b. Apply hydrogen peroxide to the wound and disinfect any instruments that have been used
    c. Continue the manicure
    d. Call the paramedics

6. The most common cause of lamellar dystrophy is
    a. injury.
    b. lack of moisture.
    c. disease.
    d. malnutrition.

7. When is the best time to file a nail?
    a. After applying nail polish
    b. While nail polish is being applied
    c. Before it has been soaked in water or oil
    d. After it has been soaked in water or oil

8. Which of the following activities takes place last in a standard pedicure?
    a. Massage
    b. Old nail polish is removed
    c. Feet are bathed in warm water
    d. Toenails are filed with an emery board

9. The outermost layer of the skin is the
    a. dermis.
    b. epidermis.
    c. subcutaneous layer.
    d. subdermis.

10. Which fingernail shape do most men have?
    a. Round
    b. Oval
    c. Almond
    d. Square

11. Which type of files should be used for an all-natural nail?
    a. Very fine
    b. Fine
    c. Medium
    d. Coarse

12. Why should fast-drying nail polishes be avoided?
    a. They tend to wash off in water.
    b. They are not available in a wide array of colors.
    c. They tend to chip more easily.
    d. They are toxic.

13. Which vitamin supplement will remedy ridges along the base of the nail bed?
    a. Vitamin A
    b. Vitamin B
    c. Vitamin C
    d. Vitamin D

14. In which direction should a nail technician file nail edges?
    a. In the direction opposite to growth
    b. Diagonally
    c. Randomly
    d. In the direction of growth

15. How should the back and wrist be positioned while administering a pedicure?
    a. The back should be straight and the wrist should be bent.
    b. The back should be bent and the wrist should be straight.
    c. Both the back and the wrist should be bent.
    d. Both the back and wrist should be straight.

16. Where are chilblains most likely to appear?
    a. The bigger toes
    b. The smaller toes
    c. The bottom of the foot
    d. The top of the foot

17. Which household product can be used to remove ink stains from nail polish?

   a. Toothpaste
   b. Vinegar
   c. Salt
   d. Flour

18. In a typical manicure, which of the following activities occurs first?

   a. Shaping of nails
   b. Application of cuticle cream
   c. Trimming of cuticles
   d. Application of liquid polish

19. The abnormal adhesion of skin to the nail plate is known as

   a. koilonychia.
   b. pterygium.
   c. psoriasis.
   d. habit tic.

20. Which type of nail backing is typically the most expensive?

   a. Mylar
   b. paper
   c. foam
   d. cloth

21. Which of the following supplies would not be subject to OSHA regulations with regard to its disposal?

   a. Emery boards
   b. Orange wood sticks
   c. Gauze
   d. Cuticle scissors

22. The white crescent at the base of a nail is called the

   a. lunula.
   b. matrix.
   c. cuticle.
   d. furrow.

23. Which nail shape produces the least risk of breakage?

   a. Oval
   b. Square
   c. Triangular
   d. None of the above

24. Which type of nail art brush is best for detail work?

   a. Shading brush
   b. Liner brush
   c. Long striping brush
   d. Fan brush

25. How often should cuticles be trimmed?
    a. Once a day
    b. Twice a day
    c. Once a week
    d. Once a month

26. Which of the following conditions can be remedied with a salt scrub?
    a. Muscle fatigue
    b. Achy joints
    c. Fluid retention
    d. All of the above

27. Which is the most common type of fingerprint pattern?
    a. Accidental
    b. Whorl
    c. Arch
    d. Loop

28. Which of the following is the least sanitary way to dispense creams or lotions?
    a. Pump
    b. Spray
    c. Finger
    d. Disposable spatula

29. What is the most likely reason for blue nails?
    a. Injury
    b. Malnutrition
    c. Poor circulation
    d. Disease

30. Which type of nail service is most likely to cause an allergic reaction?
    a. Nail enhancement
    b. Manicure
    c. Pedicure
    d. Paraffin wax treatment

31. Which of these statements is true?
    a. Dorsal skin is more sensitive than volar skin.
    b. Volar skin is more flexible than dorsal skin.
    c. Volar skin is on the back of the hand, and dorsal skin is on the palm.
    d. Dorsal skin is on the back of the hand, and volar skin is on the palm.

32. What should be used to remove the adhesive left behind by the guide strips used during a French manicure?
    a. Nail polish remover
    b. A cotton ball soaked in alcohol
    c. Lotion
    d. Soap and water

33. In a traditional French manicure, the tip of the nail is
    a. black.
    b. square.
    c. white.
    d. pointed.

34. Which of the following is not a contaminant typically found in nail adhesives?
    a. Camphor
    b. Polyvinyl butyral
    c. Dibutyl phthalate
    d. Hydroquinone

35. Inflammation of the bottom of the heel is called
    a. heel spur.
    b. bursitis.
    c. heel bump.
    d. gout.

36. The bones of the fingers are also known as
    a. ulnas.
    b. metatarsals.
    c. metacarpals.
    d. phalanges.

37. Which of the following removes nail polish?
    a. Acetic acid
    b. Acetylated lanolin
    c. Acetyl tributyl citrate
    d. Acetone

38. Employers are made responsible for maintaining healthy indoor air quality by the General Duty Clause of the
    a. Safety and Wellness Act.
    b. Occupational Safety and Health Act.
    c. Cosmetology Enforcement Act.
    d. Industrial Hygiene Act.

39. Which of the following types of corn is the most common?
    a. Vascular corn
    b. Fibrous corn
    c. Seed corn
    d. Hard corn

40. Which of the following solvents may be toxic if used repeatedly?
    a. Toluene
    b. Propylene carbonate
    c. Methylpropanediol
    d. Isododecane

41. Which of the following manicures typically takes the longest?
    a. Traditional French manicure
    b. Regular manicure for acrylic nails
    c. American manicure
    d. Basic manicure

42. In massage, quickly and lightly striking the body is known as
    a. effleurage.
    b. friction.
    c. petrissage.
    d. tapotement.

43. What is the purpose of the safety data sheet for a disinfectant?
    a. It indicates who is allowed to use the product.
    b. It describes the safe use and storage for the product.
    c. It lists the ingredients of the product.
    d. It lists the products with which the disinfectant should not be mixed.

44. What is the main difference between gel and acrylic nails?
    a. Gel nails are more flexible.
    b. Gel nails are more durable.
    c. Gel nails contain both a monomer liquid and a polymer powder.
    d. Acrylic nails contain both a polymer powder.

45. What is the first step in cleaning a file that can be submerged in water?
    a. The file should be wiped with a paper towel.
    b. The file should be dried.
    c. The file should be rinsed.
    d. The file should be cleaned with a stiff brush.

46. According to the OSHA Universal Precautions, who is responsible for making sure that employees use appropriate personal protective equipment?
    a. Employee
    b. Employer
    c. Client
    d. Local government

47. Which one of the following is a common and potentially dangerous component of nail primer?
    a. Acetonitrile
    b. Formaldehyde
    c. Methacrylic acid
    d. Phthalates

48. Which one of the following condition should be treated by a nail technician?
    a. Callus
    b. Ingrown toenail
    c. Hangnail
    d. Corn

49. What should be done to the nail surface before wrapping?

    a. The surface should be roughened.
    b. The surface should be smoothed.
    c. The surface should be polished.
    d. The surface should be massaged.

50. What is the standard procedure for giving a pedicure to a client with athlete's foot?

    a. The nail technician should not trim the cuticles.
    b. The nail technician should wear rubber gloves.
    c. The client's feet should be washed first.
    d. The client should not be given a pedicure.

Answer Key and Explanations

1 A: Clean metal implements used for nail care should be stored in a jar with sanitizing liquid. There is special sanitizing liquid available for nail technicians. Placing metal implements in a sanitizing liquid maintains sterility and impedes the spread of disease. The nail technician's workspace should also include some sanitized towels and fresh emery boards.

2. C: Horizontal lines on the nail plate are known as Beau's lines. These lines often appear after injury, or as a result of malnutrition. The hyponychium is the edge of the nail bed that forms a seal against the nail plate. Leukonychia is a condition in which white dots or streaks appear on the nail. Koilonychia is a condition in which the nail is irregularly shaped. This condition, which is caused by anemia, presents as a thin nail that curves inwards.

3. C: The highest temperature at which flammable nail products should be stored is 120°F. Nail products such as enamels, lacquers, and polish removers are extremely flammable. These products should always be covered and kept in containers when they are not in use, and they should be kept away from open flames, sparks, heat sources, and direct sunlight.

4. B: The purpose of a paraffin treatment for the hands is to improve the absorption of lotion. In a paraffin treatment, the hands are dipped repeatedly into melted paraffin wax. The repeated submergence of the hand creates a thick coat, which warms the skin of the hand for a long time and makes it unlikely that the paraffin coat will fracture before the treatment is finished. Once the hands have been dipped in wax several times and the coating has dried sufficiently, the hands will be wrapped in plastic or aluminum foil and cloth, to further lock in the heat.

5. B: If blood is drawn during a manicure, the nail technician should apply hydrogen peroxide to the wound and disinfect any instruments that have been used. Alternatively, the technician may use powdered alum to disinfect the area. In any case, the manicure should not continue until both the client and any instruments that were being used have been thoroughly disinfected. It is not necessary to send the client home or call the paramedics, however, unless the severity of the client's injury warrants such measures.

6. B: The most common cause of lamellar dystrophy is lack of moisture. Lamellar dystrophy is a common condition in which the nails peel or flake. The typical treatment for lamellar dystrophy is to file the nails gently with a very fine emery board. The nails and cuticles should then be moisturized. A client who has lamellar dystrophy should be advised to apply nail oil at least once a day.

7. C: The best time to file a nail is before it has been soaked in water or oil. Nails are easiest to file when they are hardest. If the nail has been soaked in water or oil, it will be much more flexible, and it will be more difficult for the technician to achieve the desired shape. Moreover, excessive hydration may cause the layers of the nail to separate, which can also make filing difficult.

8. A: In a standard pedicure, a massage takes place after the other activities listed. The standard pedicure begins with the removal of the client's shoes and socks. The nail technician will then examine the client's feet, and bathe them in warm water. Next, the technician will remove any old nail polish, and will file the toenails with an emery board. The technician will then use an orange wood stick to loosen the cuticles. The feet are then rinsed and dried, and cuticle cream is applied to the toes. The feet are washed again in warm soap and water, and the massage is administered. Finally, the technician will apply nail polish and sealant.

9. B: The outermost layer of the skin is the epidermis. This layer of skin is the first line of defense for the body. It is slightly acidic, which repels some harmful substances and retains moisture. Beneath the epidermis lies the dermis, a sponge-like layer of connective tissue. The dermis is primarily composed of collagen and elastin. The innermost layer of the skin is known as the subcutaneous layer. It is mainly made up of fat and large blood vessels.

10. A: Most men have a round fingernail shape. A rounded shape is appropriate for shorter nails. The oval shape is also rounded, but it has a slightly more pronounced arch. This shape is common for women with short or medium length nails. The almond shape is even more pointed; it has a tendency to make the fingers look stubby. A square shape is common for long nails.

11. A: A very fine file should be used for an all-natural nail. Natural nails are very susceptible to damage, so the nail technician should use the most gentle files and Emery boards available. This will prevent damage to the edge of the nail, or separation of the nail layers.

12. C: Fast-drying nail polishes should be avoided because they tend to chip more easily. It is not difficult to repair chipped nail polish, but an ounce of prevention is worth a pound of cure. If a manicure chips more than a week after the polish was originally applied, it is most likely time for a new manicure anyway. To repair chipped nail polish, the nail technician will place nail polish remover on his or her index finger, and then rub this finger over the chip to remove any rough edges. After the nail polish remover has dried, the technician will spread a small amount of polish onto the chipped area, over which a coat of transparent nail polish or polish sealant will be applied to reduce the risk of shipping in the future. The area should then be cleaned with a cotton ball and nail polish remover.

13. B: Vitamin B supplements will remedy ridges along the base of the nail bed. In general, vitamin D is effective for improving the health of nails and cuticles. Vitamin A is an effective antioxidant, and can be quite good for the skin. Vitamin C is also an effective antioxidant, and can be used topically to diminish sun damage and improve healing. Vitamin D is somewhat important for nail health, but it can be obtained from moderate sun exposure.

14. D: A nail technician should file nail edges in the direction of growth. This reduces the risk of scratching or splitting the nail plate. Moreover, filing this direction will reduce the client's sensitivity to the nail adhesive. A nail technician should also use a flat file, and should consider the client's medical history and sensitivities.

15. D: While administering a pedicure, both the back and the wrist should be straight. This is the best way to avoid ergonomic problems related to repetitive movement. The nail technician's back should be kept straight regardless of whether he or she is working on a low stool or kneeling on the floor. The wrist should be kept straight during both buffing and filing.

16. B: Chilblains are most likely to appear on the smaller toes. However, they may also appear on the larger toes or on areas of the feet that receive repeated pressure. Chilblains are small swollen areas on the skin. When exposed to cold or damp, they may be quite painful. It is also easy for chilblains to become infected if the skin around them should crack. The best treatment for chilblains is to warm the entire body, apply soothing lotions, and avoid scratching.

17. A: Toothpaste can be used to remove ink stains from nail polish. The toothpaste may be applied to a cotton ball or Q-tip, or may be spread on directly with the finger. The paste is rubbed into the nail, and then wiped off with a damp cloth or water.

18. A: In a typical manicure, the shaping of nails would precede the other activities. A manicure usually begins with the client and the nail technician sitting down at a table. The nail technician will then examine the client's hands and remove any old nail polish. The next step is to shape the nails, after which the cuticles are trimmed and pushed back. The technician may then clean and bleach under the nail, or may apply a whitening agent to the nail edge. The technician will then apply cuticle cream, and will clean and dry the nails. The nail edges are then filed down, and any split or broken nails are repaired. Finally, the technician will apply the nail polish, sealant, and hand lotion.

19. B: The abnormal adhesion of skin to the nail plate is known as pterygium. When this occurs, the skin will be stretched as the nail continues to grow. This condition is typically caused by damage to the base of the nail. When a client manifests this condition, the technician should not use any products containing solvents. The condition can be eased by the gentle massage of warm oil into the area. Koilonychia is a condition in which the nails are abnormally flat, thin, and soft. This condition is typically the result of anemia or excessive use of oils or soaps. Psoriasis of the nails manifests as pitting and fragility. A habit tic is a set of ridges running laterally across the nail, typically the result of nervous picking at the fold of the nail. The ridges created by habit tic should not be buffed out.

20. C: A foam nail backing is typically the most expensive. However, this type of backing also tends to be the most durable, and can be submerged in water. In a nail enhancement process, the backing is the material on which the abrasive will be mounted. A Mylar backing is also high quality, because it can be washed and submerged in water. Paper backings, on the other hand, do not last when submerged in water. Cloth backing is typically made of cotton, and is somewhat durable.

21. D: Cuticle scissors would not be subject to OSHA regulations with regard to their disposal. The Occupational Safety and Health Administration has established special rules for certain types of waste, especially waste that may be infected with blood. After being used, items such as emery boards, orange wood sticks, Q-tips, and gauze must be placed in a double bag clearly marked as biohazardous waste. Metal implements, such as cuticle scissors, must be disinfected in a tuberculocidal agent before each use.

22. A: The white crescent at the base of a nail is called the lunula. This area lies partially under the cuticle, which is the thin layer of skin tissue that extends over the bottom of the nail. The matrix is the root of the nail, and is where keratin is produced. A furrow is any ridge or corrugation along the surface of the nail.

23. B: A square nail shape produces the least risk of breakage. Most people do not like the appearance of a squared-off nail, however, so this is typically only done when necessary. For instance, after a fingernail is torn, it may be glued back together and then filed into a square. This shape provides the most structural stability.

24. B: A liner brush is best for detail work in nail art. This type of brush has the firmest and narrowest set of bristles. A shading brush is used to create texture and blend colors on the nail. A long striping brush is designed for drawing straight lines, and a fan brush is used to create a specific sweeping texture.

25. C: Cuticles should be trimmed once a week. Before they are cut, they should be softened with a special moisturizing cuticle cream. Then, the cuticles may be carefully trimmed with a clipper.

26. D: Muscle fatigue, achy joints, and fluid retention can all be remedied with a salt scrub. This procedure increases circulation and produces a more even skin tone. There are commercial salt scrubs available, but it is easy to make a serviceable scrub with lavender oil, carrier oil, and coarse

sea salt. The feet should be moistened before being exfoliated with the salt scrub. Afterward, the feet should be rinsed with warm water and patted dry.

27. D: The loop is the most common type of fingerprint pattern. In the loop pattern, all of the ridges begin on one side of the finger, extend to the other side, and then terminate back on the side on which they started. In an accidental pattern, the fingerprint seems to follow a random path, which may include arches, loops, and whorls. In a whorl pattern, the ridges form a spiral covering the entire width of the finger. In an arch pattern, the ridges run from one side of the finger to the other, rising in the center.

28. C: Using a finger is the least sanitary way to dispense creams or lotions. Whenever possible, a nail technician should use a pump or spray for these products. If these options are unavailable, the technician should use a disposable spatula. Using a finger to scoop out cream or lotion creates a very hospitable environment for bacteria.

29. C: The most likely reason for blue nails is poor circulation. This condition, as the name suggests, presents as nails with a blue or gray tinge. If a client has blue nails, it is likely that the nails will be thin and weak as well. A client with blue nails should not receive artificial nails, because the underlying nail will not be strong enough to support the enhancements. The best immediate treatment for blue nails is a vigorous hand massage, which will encourage greater circulation to the nails.

30. A: Nail enhancement is the most likely service to cause an allergic reaction. The adhesive products required for nail enhancement are the most likely culprits when a client suffers a violent allergic reaction. To minimize the risk of such a reaction, the nail technician should keep his or her work area clean, and should never reuse towels. If a liquid monomer is used in the enhancement, the technician should avoid placing this monomer in direct contact with the skin.

31. D: Dorsal skin is on the back of the hand, and volar skin is on the palm. The volar skin is much more sensitive, but less flexible, than the dorsal skin, which needs to accommodate the movements of the hand bones. The dorsal skin is covered with fine hairs, but the volar skin is hairless. The volar skin does have a large number of sebaceous glands.

32. B: A cotton ball soaked in alcohol should be used to remove the adhesive left behind by the guide strips used during a French manicure. In a French manicure, the base of the nail is a different color than the tip. Nail technicians use guide strips to help them make the stripes at the tip of the nail a consistent size. However, the guide strips often leave behind a sticky adhesive residue. The best way to remove this adhesive is to soak a cotton ball in alcohol and gently rub it across the nail.

33. C: In a traditional French manicure, the tip of the nail is white, while the body of the nail is a neutral color. The original intention of the French manicure was to make the nail appear healthy and clean. Now, many clients will request a French manicure with different colors.

34. A: Camphor is not a contaminant typically found in nail adhesives. This solvent is a common ingredient in lacquers and top coats. The other three answer choices are all chemicals commonly found in nail adhesives. All of these chemicals have been listed as air contaminants by the Occupational Safety and Health Administration. Acetone is the most common air contaminant in nail adhesives, nail polish, and nail polish remover.

35. B: Inflammation of the bottom of the heel is called bursitis. Heel bursitis is the result of persistent irritation of the heel, typically as a result of excessive use or rheumatoid arthritis. Gout may be associated with bursitis, though it is typically more of a general swelling of the entire ankle

area. A heel spur is an abnormal growth of the bone itself. This condition, which is caused by the formation of calcium deposits, can be very painful. Heel bumps appear on the back of the heel, particularly where the bone attaches to the Achilles tendon. Heel bumps are typically the result of shoe friction.

36. D: The bones of the fingers are also known as phalanges. There are fourteen phalanges in each of the hands. The hand contains five bones, known as metacarpals. The metatarsals are the long bones in the feet. The ulna is the outside bone of the forearm when the arm is positioned with the palm down.

37. D: Acetone removes nail polish. It is an extremely strong solvent. Acetic acid is generally irritating to the body; it is commonly found in vinegar and some fruits. Acetylated lanolin is an emollient created by the sebaceous glands of sheep. It is an extremely effective moisturizer for the skin. Acetyl tributyl citrate is commonly used as a plasticizer in nail polish and other products used to harden nails.

38. B: Employers are made responsible for maintaining healthy indoor air quality by the General Duty Clause of the Occupational Safety and Health Act. This means that the employer is responsible for ensuring that the workplace has proper ventilation and that air contaminants are not allowed to linger in the work environment.

39. D: Of the given types of corn, hard corns are the most common. Corns are accumulations of dead skin on the hands or feet. They are caused by repetitive pressure or friction. Corns, unlike calluses, are typically located over bones or joints. A hard corn is typically cone-shaped, with a defined nucleus in the center. A vascular corn may be hard or soft, but it contains a blood vessel. Vascular corns may be very painful, and may bleed quite a bit if cut. A fibrous corn occurs when a corn has been present for a very long time. These corns are often painful, in part because they are more deeply rooted in the skin. A seed corn is typically very small, though seed corns may appear in clusters. These corns are painless for the most part.

40. A: Toluene may be toxic if used repeatedly. Propylene carbonate is also used as a film-forming agent, meaning that it creates a continuous covering wherever it is applied. Methylpropanediol is a glycol solvent that improves the penetration of moisturizing ingredients into the skin. Isododecane is a hydrocarbon-based product that is very light and improves the ability of other chemicals to spread across the body.

41. B: Of the given types of manicure, the regular manicure for acrylic nails will typically take the longest. This process lasts an average of one hour and fifteen minutes. The basic manicure should only take about half an hour, and a traditional French or American manicure should take between 45 minutes and an hour.

42. D: In massage, quickly and lightly striking the body is known as tapotement. Tapotement may be adjusted by changing the way the hand is shaped. For instance, the technician may use a chopping motion with the side of the hand, or may cup the hand and strike with the palm down. Effleurage is a long stroke with moderate pressure, usually administered along the length of the muscle. Friction is vigorous rubbing of the muscles. Pétrissage is kneading, either with the fists or the fingers.

43. B: The purpose of the safety data sheet for a disinfectant is to describe the safe use and storage for the product. The Occupational Safety and Health Administration has established guidelines for the drafting and dissemination of safety data sheets. Any substances that are potentially harmful

must be accompanied by a safety data sheet, and this information must also be accessible to local fire departments and emergency services personnel.

44. A: The main difference between gel and acrylic nails is that gel nails are more flexible. Both gel nails and acrylic nails contain a monomer liquid and a polymer powder. Either style of nail can be styled long or short.

45. D: The first step in cleaning a file that can be submerged in water is to clean it with a stiff brush. Files that can be submerged in water are reusable, but they need to be cleaned properly. The first step is to brush away all the dust from the file. The file should then be rinsed and placed in a disinfectant for the interval indicated on the safety data sheet. The file may then be taken out of the disinfectant, rinsed, and dried between clean paper towels. When it is not in use, a reusable file should be kept in a container with a lid.

46. B: According to the OSHA Universal Precautions, the employer is responsible for making sure that employees use appropriate personal protective equipment. If the employee declines to wear such equipment as is necessary to eliminate a reasonable risk of harm, the employer should be able to prove that the failure to wear this equipment was the decision of the employee.

47. C: Methacrylic acid is a common and potentially dangerous component of nail primer. If this substance is not washed off the nail relatively soon after application, it can cause skin irritation. Acetonitrile is the primary ingredient in artificial nail removers. It should be kept out of the reach of children. Formaldehyde is often found in nail hardeners. This chemical, which may be referred to as methylene glycol or formalin on packaging, is an irritant and has been to blame for severe allergic reactions. Phthalates are often found in nail polish as a strengthening agent. They may be damaging to health when exposure is prolonged.

48. C: Hangnails should be treated by a nail technician. The typical strategy for dealing with a hangnail is to trim it as short as possible, and then use a file to smooth down the base of the hangnail. It may be necessary to trim the cuticle to prevent the return of a hangnail.

49. A: The nail surface should be roughened before wrapping. The roughing process enables the adhesive to function much more effectively. An emery board or coarse file can be used to rough up the nail plate.

50. D: A client with athlete's foot should not be given a pedicure. Athlete's foot is a highly contagious fungal infection. It can easily be spread by contact with other people and with the instruments used during a pedicure. A client who has athlete's foot should be referred to a physician, and should have the fungus eliminated before receiving a pedicure.

How to Overcome Test Anxiety

Just the thought of taking a test is enough to make most people a little nervous. A test is an important event that can have a long-term impact on your future, so it's important to take it seriously and it's natural to feel anxious about performing well. But just because anxiety is normal, that doesn't mean that it's helpful in test taking, or that you should simply accept it as part of your life. Anxiety can have a variety of effects. These effects can be mild, like making you feel slightly nervous, or severe, like blocking your ability to focus or remember even a simple detail.

If you experience test anxiety—whether severe or mild—it's important to know how to beat it. To discover this, first you need to understand what causes test anxiety.

Causes of Test Anxiety

While we often think of anxiety as an uncontrollable emotional state, it can actually be caused by simple, practical things. One of the most common causes of test anxiety is that a person does not feel adequately prepared for their test. This feeling can be the result of many different issues such as poor study habits or lack of organization, but the most common culprit is time management. Starting to study too late, failing to organize your study time to cover all of the material, or being distracted while you study will mean that you're not well prepared for the test. This may lead to cramming the night before, which will cause you to be physically and mentally exhausted for the test. Poor time management also contributes to feelings of stress, fear, and hopelessness as you realize you are not well prepared but don't know what to do about it.

Other times, test anxiety is not related to your preparation for the test but comes from unresolved fear. This may be a past failure on a test, or poor performance on tests in general. It may come from comparing yourself to others who seem to be performing better or from the stress of living up to expectations. Anxiety may be driven by fears of the future—how failure on this test would affect your educational and career goals. These fears are often completely irrational, but they can still negatively impact your test performance.

> **Review Video:** <u>3 Reasons You Have Test Anxiety</u>
> Visit mometrix.com/academy and enter code: 428468

Elements of Test Anxiety

As mentioned earlier, test anxiety is considered to be an emotional state, but it has physical and mental components as well. Sometimes you may not even realize that you are suffering from test anxiety until you notice the physical symptoms. These can include trembling hands, rapid heartbeat, sweating, nausea, and tense muscles. Extreme anxiety may lead to fainting or vomiting. Obviously, any of these symptoms can have a negative impact on testing. It is important to recognize them as soon as they begin to occur so that you can address the problem before it damages your performance.

> **Review Video: 3 Ways to Tell You Have Test Anxiety**
> Visit mometrix.com/academy and enter code: 927847

The mental components of test anxiety include trouble focusing and inability to remember learned information. During a test, your mind is on high alert, which can help you recall information and stay focused for an extended period of time. However, anxiety interferes with your mind's natural processes, causing you to blank out, even on the questions you know well. The strain of testing during anxiety makes it difficult to stay focused, especially on a test that may take several hours. Extreme anxiety can take a huge mental toll, making it difficult not only to recall test information but even to understand the test questions or pull your thoughts together.

> **Review Video: How Test Anxiety Affects Memory**
> Visit mometrix.com/academy and enter code: 609003

Effects of Test Anxiety

Test anxiety is like a disease—if left untreated, it will get progressively worse. Anxiety leads to poor performance, and this reinforces the feelings of fear and failure, which in turn lead to poor performances on subsequent tests. It can grow from a mild nervousness to a crippling condition. If allowed to progress, test anxiety can have a big impact on your schooling, and consequently on your future.

Test anxiety can spread to other parts of your life. Anxiety on tests can become anxiety in any stressful situation, and blanking on a test can turn into panicking in a job situation. But fortunately, you don't have to let anxiety rule your testing and determine your grades. There are a number of relatively simple steps you can take to move past anxiety and function normally on a test and in the rest of life.

> **Review Video: How Test Anxiety Impacts Your Grades**
> Visit mometrix.com/academy and enter code: 939819

Physical Steps for Beating Test Anxiety

While test anxiety is a serious problem, the good news is that it can be overcome. It doesn't have to control your ability to think and remember information. While it may take time, you can begin taking steps today to beat anxiety.

Just as your first hint that you may be struggling with anxiety comes from the physical symptoms, the first step to treating it is also physical. Rest is crucial for having a clear, strong mind. If you are tired, it is much easier to give in to anxiety. But if you establish good sleep habits, your body and mind will be ready to perform optimally, without the strain of exhaustion. Additionally, sleeping well helps you to retain information better, so you're more likely to recall the answers when you see the test questions.

Getting good sleep means more than going to bed on time. It's important to allow your brain time to relax. Take study breaks from time to time so it doesn't get overworked, and don't study right before bed. Take time to rest your mind before trying to rest your body, or you may find it difficult to fall asleep.

> **Review Video: The Importance of Sleep for Your Brain**
> Visit mometrix.com/academy and enter code: 319338

Along with sleep, other aspects of physical health are important in preparing for a test. Good nutrition is vital for good brain function. Sugary foods and drinks may give a burst of energy but this burst is followed by a crash, both physically and emotionally. Instead, fuel your body with protein and vitamin-rich foods.

Also, drink plenty of water. Dehydration can lead to headaches and exhaustion, especially if your brain is already under stress from the rigors of the test. Particularly if your test is a long one, drink water during the breaks. And if possible, take an energy-boosting snack to eat between sections.

> **Review Video: How Diet Can Affect your Mood**
> Visit mometrix.com/academy and enter code: 624317

Along with sleep and diet, a third important part of physical health is exercise. Maintaining a steady workout schedule is helpful, but even taking 5-minute study breaks to walk can help get your blood pumping faster and clear your head. Exercise also releases endorphins, which contribute to a positive feeling and can help combat test anxiety.

When you nurture your physical health, you are also contributing to your mental health. If your body is healthy, your mind is much more likely to be healthy as well. So take time to rest, nourish your body with healthy food and water, and get moving as much as possible. Taking these physical steps will make you stronger and more able to take the mental steps necessary to overcome test anxiety.

> **Review Video: How to Stay Healthy and Prevent Test Anxiety**
> Visit mometrix.com/academy and enter code: 877894

Mental Steps for Beating Test Anxiety

Working on the mental side of test anxiety can be more challenging, but as with the physical side, there are clear steps you can take to overcome it. As mentioned earlier, test anxiety often stems from lack of preparation, so the obvious solution is to prepare for the test. Effective studying may be the most important weapon you have for beating test anxiety, but you can and should employ several other mental tools to combat fear.

First, boost your confidence by reminding yourself of past success—tests or projects that you aced. If you're putting as much effort into preparing for this test as you did for those, there's no reason you should expect to fail here. Work hard to prepare; then trust your preparation.

Second, surround yourself with encouraging people. It can be helpful to find a study group, but be sure that the people you're around will encourage a positive attitude. If you spend time with others who are anxious or cynical, this will only contribute to your own anxiety. Look for others who are motivated to study hard from a desire to succeed, not from a fear of failure.

Third, reward yourself. A test is physically and mentally tiring, even without anxiety, and it can be helpful to have something to look forward to. Plan an activity following the test, regardless of the outcome, such as going to a movie or getting ice cream.

When you are taking the test, if you find yourself beginning to feel anxious, remind yourself that you know the material. Visualize successfully completing the test. Then take a few deep, relaxing breaths and return to it. Work through the questions carefully but with confidence, knowing that you are capable of succeeding.

Developing a healthy mental approach to test taking will also aid in other areas of life. Test anxiety affects more than just the actual test—it can be damaging to your mental health and even contribute to depression. It's important to beat test anxiety before it becomes a problem for more than testing.

> **Review Video: Test Anxiety and Depression**
> Visit mometrix.com/academy and enter code: 904704

Study Strategy

Being prepared for the test is necessary to combat anxiety, but what does being prepared look like? You may study for hours on end and still not feel prepared. What you need is a strategy for test prep. The next few pages outline our recommended steps to help you plan out and conquer the challenge of preparation.

Step 1: Scope Out the Test

Learn everything you can about the format (multiple choice, essay, etc.) and what will be on the test. Gather any study materials, course outlines, or sample exams that may be available. Not only will this help you to prepare, but knowing what to expect can help to alleviate test anxiety.

Step 2: Map Out the Material

Look through the textbook or study guide and make note of how many chapters or sections it has. Then divide these over the time you have. For example, if a book has 15 chapters and you have five days to study, you need to cover three chapters each day. Even better, if you have the time, leave an extra day at the end for overall review after you have gone through the material in depth.

If time is limited, you may need to prioritize the material. Look through it and make note of which sections you think you already have a good grasp on, and which need review. While you are studying, skim quickly through the familiar sections and take more time on the challenging parts. Write out your plan so you don't get lost as you go. Having a written plan also helps you feel more in control of the study, so anxiety is less likely to arise from feeling overwhelmed at the amount to cover. A sample plan may look like this:

- Day 1: Skim chapters 1–4, study chapter 5 (especially pages 31–33)
- Day 2: Study chapters 6–7, skim chapters 8–9
- Day 3: Skim chapter 10, study chapters 11–12 (especially pages 87–90)
- Day 4: Study chapters 13–15
- Day 5: Overall review (focus most on chapters 5, 6, and 12), take practice test

Step 3: Gather Your Tools

Decide what study method works best for you. Do you prefer to highlight in the book as you study and then go back over the highlighted portions? Or do you type out notes of the important information? Or is it helpful to make flashcards that you can carry with you? Assemble the pens, index cards, highlighters, post-it notes, and any other materials you may need so you won't be distracted by getting up to find things while you study.

If you're having a hard time retaining the information or organizing your notes, experiment with different methods. For example, try color-coding by subject with colored pens, highlighters, or post-it notes. If you learn better by hearing, try recording yourself reading your notes so you can listen while in the car, working out, or simply sitting at your desk. Ask a friend to quiz you from your flashcards, or try teaching someone the material to solidify it in your mind.

Step 4: Create Your Environment

It's important to avoid distractions while you study. This includes both the obvious distractions like visitors and the subtle distractions like an uncomfortable chair (or a too-comfortable couch that makes you want to fall asleep). Set up the best study environment possible: good lighting and a comfortable work area. If background music helps you focus, you may want to turn it on, but otherwise keep the room quiet. If you are using a computer to take notes, be sure you don't have any other windows open, especially applications like social media, games, or anything else that could distract you. Silence your phone and turn off notifications. Be sure to keep water close by so you stay hydrated while you study (but avoid unhealthy drinks and snacks).

Also, take into account the best time of day to study. Are you freshest first thing in the morning? Try to set aside some time then to work through the material. Is your mind clearer in the afternoon or evening? Schedule your study session then. Another method is to study at the same time of day that you will take the test, so that your brain gets used to working on the material at that time and will be ready to focus at test time.

Step 5: Study!

Once you have done all the study preparation, it's time to settle into the actual studying. Sit down, take a few moments to settle your mind so you can focus, and begin to follow your study plan. Don't give in to distractions or let yourself procrastinate. This is your time to prepare so you'll be ready to fearlessly approach the test. Make the most of the time and stay focused.

Of course, you don't want to burn out. If you study too long you may find that you're not retaining the information very well. Take regular study breaks. For example, taking five minutes out of every hour to walk briskly, breathing deeply and swinging your arms, can help your mind stay fresh.

As you get to the end of each chapter or section, it's a good idea to do a quick review. Remind yourself of what you learned and work on any difficult parts. When you feel that you've mastered the material, move on to the next part. At the end of your study session, briefly skim through your notes again.

But while review is helpful, cramming last minute is NOT. If at all possible, work ahead so that you won't need to fit all your study into the last day. Cramming overloads your brain with more information than it can process and retain, and your tired mind may struggle to recall even previously learned information when it is overwhelmed with last-minute study. Also, the urgent nature of cramming and the stress placed on your brain contribute to anxiety. You'll be more likely to go to the test feeling unprepared and having trouble thinking clearly.

So don't cram, and don't stay up late before the test, even just to review your notes at a leisurely pace. Your brain needs rest more than it needs to go over the information again. In fact, plan to finish your studies by noon or early afternoon the day before the test. Give your brain the rest of the day to relax or focus on other things, and get a good night's sleep. Then you will be fresh for the test and better able to recall what you've studied.

Step 6: Take a practice test

Many courses offer sample tests, either online or in the study materials. This is an excellent resource to check whether you have mastered the material, as well as to prepare for the test format and environment.

Check the test format ahead of time: the number of questions, the type (multiple choice, free response, etc.), and the time limit. Then create a plan for working through them. For example, if you have 30 minutes to take a 60-question test, your limit is 30 seconds per question. Spend less time on the questions you know well so that you can take more time on the difficult ones.

If you have time to take several practice tests, take the first one open book, with no time limit. Work through the questions at your own pace and make sure you fully understand them. Gradually work up to taking a test under test conditions: sit at a desk with all study materials put away and set a timer. Pace yourself to make sure you finish the test with time to spare and go back to check your answers if you have time.

After each test, check your answers. On the questions you missed, be sure you understand why you missed them. Did you misread the question (tests can use tricky wording)? Did you forget the information? Or was it something you hadn't learned? Go back and study any shaky areas that the practice tests reveal.

Taking these tests not only helps with your grade, but also aids in combating test anxiety. If you're already used to the test conditions, you're less likely to worry about it, and working through tests until you're scoring well gives you a confidence boost. Go through the practice tests until you feel comfortable, and then you can go into the test knowing that you're ready for it.

Test Tips

On test day, you should be confident, knowing that you've prepared well and are ready to answer the questions. But aside from preparation, there are several test day strategies you can employ to maximize your performance.

First, as stated before, get a good night's sleep the night before the test (and for several nights before that, if possible). Go into the test with a fresh, alert mind rather than staying up late to study.

Try not to change too much about your normal routine on the day of the test. It's important to eat a nutritious breakfast, but if you normally don't eat breakfast at all, consider eating just a protein bar. If you're a coffee drinker, go ahead and have your normal coffee. Just make sure you time it so that the caffeine doesn't wear off right in the middle of your test. Avoid sugary beverages, and drink enough water to stay hydrated but not so much that you need a restroom break 10 minutes into the test. If your test isn't first thing in the morning, consider going for a walk or doing a light workout before the test to get your blood flowing.

Allow yourself enough time to get ready, and leave for the test with plenty of time to spare so you won't have the anxiety of scrambling to arrive in time. Another reason to be early is to select a good seat. It's helpful to sit away from doors and windows, which can be distracting. Find a good seat, get out your supplies, and settle your mind before the test begins.

When the test begins, start by going over the instructions carefully, even if you already know what to expect. Make sure you avoid any careless mistakes by following the directions.

Then begin working through the questions, pacing yourself as you've practiced. If you're not sure on an answer, don't spend too much time on it, and don't let it shake your confidence. Either skip it and come back later, or eliminate as many wrong answers as possible and guess among the remaining ones. Don't dwell on these questions as you continue—put them out of your mind and focus on what lies ahead.

Be sure to read all of the answer choices, even if you're sure the first one is the right answer. Sometimes you'll find a better one if you keep reading. But don't second-guess yourself if you do immediately know the answer. Your gut instinct is usually right. Don't let test anxiety rob you of the information you know.

If you have time at the end of the test (and if the test format allows), go back and review your answers. Be cautious about changing any, since your first instinct tends to be correct, but make sure you didn't misread any of the questions or accidentally mark the wrong answer choice. Look over any you skipped and make an educated guess.

At the end, leave the test feeling confident. You've done your best, so don't waste time worrying about your performance or wishing you could change anything. Instead, celebrate the successful completion of this test. And finally, use this test to learn how to deal with anxiety even better next time.

> **Review Video: 5 Tips to Beat Test Anxiety**
> Visit mometrix.com/academy and enter code: 570656

Important Qualification

Not all anxiety is created equal. If your test anxiety is causing major issues in your life beyond the classroom or testing center, or if you are experiencing troubling physical symptoms related to your anxiety, it may be a sign of a serious physiological or psychological condition. If this sounds like your situation, we strongly encourage you to seek professional help.

Thank You

We at Mometrix would like to extend our heartfelt thanks to you, our friend and patron, for allowing us to play a part in your journey. It is a privilege to serve people from all walks of life who are unified in their commitment to building the best future they can for themselves.

The preparation you devote to these important testing milestones may be the most valuable educational opportunity you have for making a real difference in your life. We encourage you to put your heart into it—that feeling of succeeding, overcoming, and yes, conquering will be well worth the hours you've invested.

We want to hear your story, your struggles and your successes, and if you see any opportunities for us to improve our materials so we can help others even more effectively in the future, please share that with us as well. **The team at Mometrix would be absolutely thrilled to hear from you!** So please, send us an email (support@mometrix.com) and let's stay in touch.

If you'd like some additional help, check out these other resources we offer for your exam:

http://MometrixFlashcards.com/NailTechnician

Additional Bonus Material

Due to our efforts to try to keep this book to a manageable length, we've created a link that will give you access to all of your additional bonus material.

Please visit **https://www.mometrix.com/bonus948/nailtechnician** to access the information.